Cat

Animal
Series editor: Jonathan Burt

Already published

Crow
Boria Sax

Ant
Charlotte Sleigh

Tortoise
Peter Young

Cockroach
Marion Copeland

Dog
Susan McHugh

Oyster
Rebecca Stott

Bear
Robert E. Bieder

Rat
Jonathan Burt

Snake
Drake Stutesman

Parrot
Paul Carter

Bee
Claire Preston

Tiger
Susie Green

Whale
Joe Roman

Falcon
Helen Macdonald

Peacock
Christine E. Jackson

Fly
Steven Connor

Fox
Martin Wallen

Salmon
Peter Coates

Forthcoming . . .

Hare
Simon Carnell

Moose
Kevin Jackson

Crocodile
Richard Freeman

Spider
Katja and Sergiusz Michalski

Duck
Victoria de Rijke

Wolf
Garry Marvin

Elephant
Daniel Wylie

Pigeon
Barbara Allen

Horse
Elaine Walker

Penguin
Stephen Martin

Rhinoceros
Kelly Enright

Cat

Katharine M. Rogers

REAKTION BOOKS

Published by
REAKTION BOOKS LTD
33 Great Sutton Street
London EC1V 0DX, UK
www.reaktionbooks.co.uk

First published 2006
Copyright © Katharine M. Rogers 2006

Printed and bound in Singapore by CS Graphics

British Library Cataloguing in Publication Data
Rogers, Katharine M.
    Cat. - (Animal)
    1. Cats 2. Human-animal relationships
    I. Title
    636.8

    ISBN-13: 978 1 86189 292 8
    ISBN-10: 1 86189 292 6

Contents

1 Wildcat to Domestic Mousecatcher

When humans first evolved, they found themselves sharing their world with other animals that engaged their attention as threats, as rivals and as food. But along with these practical concerns, they were impressed by the superior strength, speed, sensory acuteness, and precise coordination they saw in so many of the animals. When humans began to express themselves artistically, in the late Paleolithic era, they drew hunts of large animals on the walls of caves. Animals fascinate us because we recognize in them consciousness, sensations, drives, and emotions like our own – yet at the same time they remain sufficiently alien that we can never hope to fully understand and communicate with them. The relationship became closer when people began to domesticate animals, starting with the dog about 14,000 years ago. They came to know these animals in a more personal way and developed deep affection for some of them, although the systematic use of creatures under their control could lead to ruthless exploitation. No matter how fond people may be of particular animals, they tend to take for granted a right to treat them as they like and use them as is convenient.

It was natural for people living in close contact with animals to look at them in human terms; comparisons usually worked to the animal's disadvantage, since it was humans who made them. People projected onto other animals the physical appetites

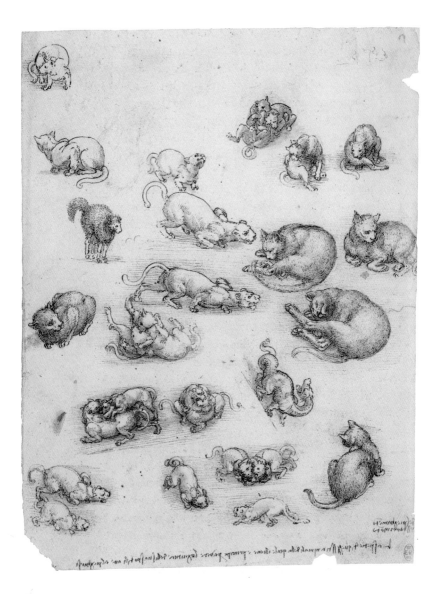

that they did not want to recognize in themselves – dogs are dirty, pigs are greedy, goats are lustful. They branded donkeys as stubborn and stupid because the animals did not always comply with their masters' unceasing demands. Even though they loved dogs more than any other animal companions, they tended to see them as inferior and appropriately less privileged versions of humans – think of the common epithets 'dog', 'cur' and 'bitch' and expressions like 'in the doghouse' and 'not fit for a dog'.

Cats, the last of the familiar domestic animals to be domesticated, have fared better than most. They have not been exploited, for people kept them to do work – catching rodent pests – that they spontaneously enjoy doing. Although they have been made emblems of sexuality, the sexuality they represent is often attractive. Their self-contained aloofness saves them from being patronized as dogs are. The same aloofness led people to credit them with uncanny abilities, which ensured them a certain respect.

On the other hand, it could lay them open to superstitious persecution: cats were commonly suspected of complicity with the devil in medieval and early modern times. Often, however, this suspicion was less the result of ideological belief than a pretext for tormenting them. Cats were readily available and esteemed of negligible value, for they did not win affection by fidelity like dogs or make substantial contributions to human welfare such as the meat of pigs and the labour of oxen. Therefore they were handy objects for organized cruelty or casual sadism. At annual ceremonies in many places, cats were burned alive to expel evil from the community. Idle soldiers in Kilkenny would amuse themselves by tying two cats together by the tail, hanging them upside down, and watching them claw each other frantically to get free; these were the originals of the cats of Kilkenny in the traditional rhyme, which describes their mutual destruction as amusing. In the 1730s, a group of apprentice printers in Paris used cats as surrogates for social superiors that they dared not attack directly. At this time cats were changing in status from utilitarian domestic assistants to pets, and it seemed to the apprentices that their employers treated their pet cats better than their employees. The apprentices expressed their resentment by formally trying and hanging the neighbourhood cats, starting with their mistress's cherished pet.[1]

Such callousness seems hard to believe in these times, when cats have come to be widely accepted as pets and valued as attractive and agreeable friends. But it is only during the last three centuries that cats have joined dogs as companion animals and members of the family. Nowadays, any references to cats' supposed uncanny powers or connection with witches are playful and affectionate. Their refusal to defer to humans like other domestic animals, which seemed wickedly insubordinate in earlier centuries, is now taken as evidence of self-respecting independence.

The paleontogical history of the cat can be traced back to the great diversification of mammals in the Paleocene epoch, at the beginning of the Cenozoic era, over 60 million years ago. The first members of its order, Carnivora, were miacids, tree-dwelling creatures that looked like pine martens and were about 20 cm (8 in) long. They did have the carnassial teeth that distinguish the Carnivora, a pair of sharpened cheek teeth that are aligned so as to work like shears in slicing meat off bone; but they had a full complement of other teeth as well and probably ate a mixed diet. For 25 million years, the dominant mammalian flesh-eaters were not Carnivora but creodonts, who also have carnassial teeth, but less efficient ones. They died out, perhaps because the miacids were better able to adapt to changing conditions.

True cats evolved from the miacid lineage about 30 million years ago; the earliest one is *Proailurus*, which weighed about 9 kg (20 lb) and resembled the modern fossa of Madagascar – a lithe animal of the civet family that hunts by leaping from branch to branch in the trees. *Proailurus* had more teeth than a modern cat and a less convoluted brain; the modern feline brain has gained mainly in the areas controlling hearing, eyesight, and limb coordination. Its descendant, *Pseudaeluris*, which evolved 20 million years ago, had teeth close to those of a modern cat but had a longer back, like a civet. It also spent more of its time in the trees than do modern cats, which have adapted to running on the ground. Two lines descended from *Pseudaeluris*, the Felinae, ancestors of all the modern cat species, and the sabre-toothed cats; and by the Pleistocene epoch (500,000 years ago), species from both groups were roaming all over Eurasia, Africa, and North America.

The sabre-tooths, the first successful large Felidae, dominated the scene through the Miocene epoch and became extinct in the Holocene, about 10,000 years ago, perhaps because their prey died out. Heavily muscled, short-legged animals who probably killed by plunging their enormous upper canines into their victim's throat, they were ideally adapted to catch large, tough-skinned prey, but were no match for the newly evolved nimble herbivores; and they lost out to faster, smarter cats. Unfortunately, we cannot trace in detail the evolution of the living species of cats, especially the small ones from whom our domestic cat is descended, because the fossil record is scanty. Their habitat, forests, was not favourable for preserving fossils. The feline species now extant all appeared within the past 10 million years: the lynx 3 to 4 million years ago, the puma 3 million years ago, the leopard 2 million years ago, and the lion 700,000 years ago. The oldest remains so far discovered of the European wildcat, an early form called *Felis sylvestris lunensis*, date from about 2 million years ago.[2]

Cats are the most specialized of all the Carnivora, the only ones who exclusively eat meat: their canine and carnassial teeth are particularly well developed, and their other teeth negligible. Their flexible, muscular bodies, acute senses, lightning reflexes and highly developed teeth and claws make them the supreme stalk-and-pounce hunters. Their flexible spines enable them to twist and turn nimbly and to reach high speed by alternately flexing and arching their backs (though this technique uses so much energy that they lack the endurance of canids and ungulates). They have long canine teeth set in powerful jaws to pierce the neck of their prey and sharp claws to grab and position it for the killing bite, as well as to climb. The small cats, which live on small prey, kill it with a very precise bite to the neck, driving their canines in between two vertebrae so that they pierce the spinal cord and thus instantly disable it from coordinating any defence. Cats have nerve endings around their canines so they can sense where to place the teeth and jaw muscles with an exceptionally short contraction time. (Canids, in contrast, cannot place their bites so precisely; on the other hand, they can crush bones, while cats can only slice flesh.) Cats keep their claws sharp by retracting them when not in use; the resultant soft paws enable the animal to steal up silently on its prey, although they are not suited to distance running. By contracting a muscle, cats can extend a tendon that protracts their claws and spreads their toes, turning their paws into a set of grappling hooks.

Cats are particularly adapted for prowling and hunting by night. With large eyes and flexible pupils that can dilate from small slits or dots in bright sunshine to circles that seem to fill

Felis sylvestris libyca, the African wild cat, ancestor of the modern domestic pet.

their eye sockets, they can see in near darkness where the light is only one-sixth as bright as humans require, without losing the capacity to protect their retinas from the full light of midday. Even when there is no light at all, they can navigate by means of hearing acute enough to detect the movements of a mouse, amplified by outer ears that rotate to pinpoint the direction of sound; a sense of smell about 30 times better than our own (though inferior to the dog's); and outer hairs, especially whiskers, that are sensitive to the slightest pressure and in effect extend their sense of touch beyond the surface of their skin. A cat fans its whiskers forward when pouncing on prey, which helps it to judge precisely where to deliver the killing bite.[3] These accomplished feline hunters soon spread over every continent except Australia and Antarctica and adapted to every habitat from mountain heights to desert, from forest to marsh to savanna.

The Felidae, from tigers to domestic cats, are remarkably similar in anatomy and habits. All are beautiful, graceful and perfectly coordinated; all are skilled and avid hunters; all are at home in the dark and most of them, including all the small cats, are solitary. They have always fascinated humans. The lion is the undisputed King of Beasts in western culture, held up as a model of grandeur and magnanimity; the tiger has been similarly admired in the Far East and the jaguar in Central and South America. Warriors in the ancient Germanic tribes, unacquainted with big cats, made the European wildcat an emblem of courage.

The wildcat, *Felis sylvestris*, is widely dispersed over Eurasia and Africa. Generally speaking, it is ferocious and untamable. However, the North African variety, *Felis sylvestris libyca*, is unusually gentle and friendly. Before 2000 BC (when its name, *miw* or *mii*, is first recorded), it was moving into ancient Egyptian villages to hunt the rats and mice that infested the grain supplies. The Egyptians were fond of animals and soon made a pet of it. Unlike all other domesticated animals, cats have changed little under human influence. Soon after domesticating wolves into dogs, humans modified them to serve as sight hounds, livestock guards, and so forth; but the cat was already superbly developed by nature to do its essential job: catching rodents. The modern cat is slightly smaller than its wild ancestor and has developed many variations in colour and length of coat. It breeds more rapidly, going through two or three reproductive cycles per year instead of one. It has become moderately social, adjusting to living in a household, and in some cases even meeting regularly with neighbourhood cats on neutral territory in a sort of feline club. It retains through life juvenile characteristics that its wild ancestors outgrow: sociability, playfulness, attachment to the original nest, and an affectionate filial attitude toward larger animals, notably humans. Nevertheless, it remains essentially independent and predatory. Writing in 1983, the zoologist Roger Tabor identified the cat as 'Britain's predominant predator'. Cats that are not socialized to humans revert to the fierce defiance of wildcats, and feral cats, unlike feral dogs, can function success- fully without human support. They are so efficient that they threaten populations of rodents, rabbits and birds, and often out- compete other small predators like foxes and raptors.[4]

From about 1450 BC, the family cat regularly appears in the party scenes represented on Egyptian tomb walls, typically sit- ting under furniture, as its descendants love to do today. It is typ- ically shown under the mistress's chair at a banquet, eagerly bit- ing into a fish or pawing at a restraining leash to get at a bowl of food. The scribe Nebamun had himself immortalized on his tomb wall doing what he liked best – hunting in the marshes with his wife, his daughter and his cat. In this highly idealized scene, where the water is packed with fish and the sky with birds and butterflies, the cat is holding three birds that it has caught.

Like many other animals in Egypt, cats were associated with a deity: Bastet, goddess of feminine allure, fertility, maternity and the home. Bastet's attributes derive naturally from the cat's grace and beauty, noisy sexuality, devoted motherhood and palpable enjoyment of the comforts of home. Originally a local goddess in the city of Bubastis, she rose to national prominence around 950 BC, when the founder of the 22nd Dynasty made Bubastis his cap- ital. From that time, images of Bastet, as an elegant seated cat or a cat-headed woman, are omnipresent in Egyptian art. The seated cats – alert yet serene, self-contained, with tail neatly curled around their paws – perfectly convey the natural feline poise and aloofness that could make a cat seem divine. Yet, because she was represented by a friendly household companion, Bastet had a par- ticular appeal for ordinary people. Herodotus, who toured Egypt in the fifth century BC, reported that Bastet's temple in Bubastis was the most attractive in the whole country and her annual festi- val the most joyous and popular. In April or May, boats crammed

The Egyptian scribe Nebamun hunting waterfowl with his wife, his daughter and his cat, depicted in a wall painting from his tomb, c. 1360 BC.

with men and women shouting bawdy songs and jokes would sail up the river to Bubastis, where they would celebrate with an orgy. It is important to remember, however, that Bastet was far from the most important animal deity in Egypt; it is modern ailurophiles who have made her predominant and seen cats as intrinsically more godlike than, say, bulls or jackals.

Statues of Bastet, the cat goddess, were common in Egypt from c. 950 BC, when a pharaoh made her the chief goddess of Egypt.

A mummified cat from Hellenistic Egypt.

Nevertheless, it is clear that the ancient Egyptians not only domesticated cats to kill rodents and snakes, but cherished them as pets. Cats regularly share in the family pleasures, and the whole family went into mourning when their cat died. Moreover, unlike all other peoples who have kept cats, the Egyptians seem to have felt no ambivalence toward their feline pets: there is no evidence that they saw anything in them that

The sun-god Ra as a cat disposing of the snake-demon Apophis in a tomb painting from 1300 BC, Deir-el-Medina.

was not pleasant and benign. Their fierce aspect was represented by the lioness-headed goddess Sekhmet.

Herodotus and later Greek visitors were particularly impressed by Egyptian cats because they had never seen such animals. To those who knew only wildcats, the sight of tame ones comfortably living in the household and responding to human affection would have been wonderful indeed. Cats spread from Egypt to Greece and then throughout the Roman Empire, but they were not conspicuous in classical times. They

A cat herding geese in a wall painting from New Kingdom Egypt.

are only occasionally mentioned in classical works of natural history. Aristotle noted that 'female cats are naturally lecherous', since they 'lure the males on to sexual intercourse, during which time they caterwaul'.[5] This observation is accurate, since the female cat does take an aggressive role in mating – yowling to gather a group of tomcats, displaying to them, and pursuing them as long as her heat continues. It also led the way to numerous later attacks on female lust that turned from cats to women. Buffon's remarkably prolonged and intense description of the female cat pursuing and forcing herself upon a reluctant male probably derived its emotional charge from apprehensions about sexually aggressive human females.

Roman coin from Rhegium, showing the city founder playing with a cat.

As often as not, however, classical scholars' remarks on cats were based on nothing more than folklore or fanciful theorizing. Perhaps inspired by the common identification of Bastet with Artemis and Diana, Plutarch misobserved the conspicuously changing pupils of cats in order to link them with the lunar cycle: cats' pupils, he claimed, 'grow large and round at the time of the full moon, and . . . become thin and narrow' when it wanes. This bit of folklore was still current in 1693, when it appeared in William Salmon's *Complete English Physician*.[6]

There is no evidence that cats were common around the houses of ancient Greece or Rome. They were not even established as the obvious controllers of rodent pests. Pliny the Elder names the weasel, not the cat, as the animal that strays 'about our homes' and chases away snakes. Both Greek *ailuros* and Latin *felis* could refer to any one of various long-tailed carnivores kept for catching mice. The specific term, *catus*, first appears in Palladius in AD 350, who proposed in his treatise on agriculture the novel idea that farmers might keep cats to chase moles from the vegetable garden, although he went on to say that weasels would do as well.[7]

Although cats occasionally appear on Greek vases or Roman mosaics, the first portrayals that express affection for them are touching Gallo-Roman monuments of the third and fourth centuries AD that show a small child clutching its beloved kitty. By the fourth century, domestic cats must have been prowling around British towns, for one left its footprints on some tiles laid out to dry beside a factory in Silchester.

Meanwhile, domestic cats were moving through Persia and India to the Far East. They were associated with evil in Zoroastrian tradition, perhaps created by the Evil Spirit and certainly treacherous, in contrast to the loyal dog, which was highly regarded. Their importance was recognized, however. Early in the seventh century, a tyrannical governor intent on destroying the city of Ray ordered that all the people's house cats be killed; the resulting plague of mice forced the inhabitants to abandon their homes, and the city was saved only when the queen brought a kitten to entertain the king and thus persuaded him to remove the wicked governor. Hostility to cats was prevalent in Persia even after the advent of Islam, which favoured them. Medieval Persian poets present them as images of greed, hypocrisy and treachery.[8] Cats were well known in India by 500 AD, when one appears in the *Pancatantra*: he is a treacherous hypocrite and thus reflects the widespread Indian suspicion of cats. Cats are not generally kept as pets in India;

The fable of 'The Mouse and the Cat' from a mid-16th-century manuscript of the *Humayunname*.

they are more apt to be seen around garbage dumps than in homes. Their habit of constantly licking themselves, signifying attractive cleanliness to westerners, is repellent to orthodox Hindus, who consider saliva unclean.

Cats probably arrived in China early in the Common Era and were certainly well known there by the Tang Dynasty. A Tang poet tells how the Empress Wu Tse-t'ien tried to demonstrate her success in enforcing Buddha's law of nonviolence throughout China by raising a kitten and a bird to eat from the same dish. Unfortunately, when they were exhibited at court, the supposedly reformed cat became nervous and killed her erstwhile comrade. In about 1000, the poet Wang Chih wrote that the scholar Chang Tuan cherished seven valuable cats, who had names like White

Kitten by Li Di (1110–97), ink and colour on silk album leaf.

Anonymous Song painting, *Cat among the Peonies*. Ink and colour, hanging scroll.

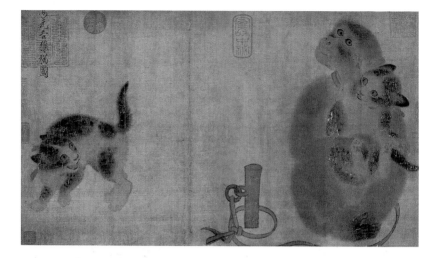

A monkey holds the kitten it has seized while another kitten looks on, wanting to attack but afraid to. Yi Yuanqui, *Cats and Monkey*, c. 1064, ink and colour on silk album leaf.

A print by Hiroshige shows a bob-tailed cat in a courtesan's window.

Phoenix and Drive-Away-Vexation.[9] Chinese artists in the Tang and Song periods created far more realistic and attractive portrayals of cats than did their medieval contemporaries in Europe.

Introduced into Japan probably around the seventh century, from China via Korea, cats were at first the rare and prized pets of court aristocrats. It was appropriate to present a cat to the emperor, and the court lady who wrote *Sarashina Diary* recorded the death of her cat along with those of her sister and husband. A comment in Murasaki Shikibu's *The Tale of Genji* (early eleventh century) shows how cats were customarily treated in court circles: 'The most unsociable cat, when it finds itself wrapped up in someone's coat and put to sleep upon his bed – stroked, fed, and tended with every imaginable care – soon ceases to stand upon its dignity.' The Crown Prince had a passion for cats and was happy to converse about them for any length of time.[10] Cats soon multiplied, of course, but they continued to be treated with respect. They were highly valued throughout the Far East for killing the

rats that destroyed not only foodstuffs but silkworm cocoons.

They were and are cherished in Thailand, where they were kept in monasteries and credited with preserving the sacred texts from being gnawed by rodents. From early times up to the present, Buddhist abbots have bred special strains of cats and refused to sell the kittens, but would only give them to people they approved. To this day, children in Thai schools regularly sing a song praising cats for their amiability and helpfulness:

O cat, kitty cat	of such lively form
Call kitty, kitty and it comes	cutely rubbing your legs
Knows how to bring love	in the evenings catching mice
Should be considered grateful	should follow its example[11]

Thus children are systematically taught to be kind to cats, and cats are held up as a model of making oneself useful.

Cats were brought to the Americas by the first European settlers in the seventeenth century. Even now cats in New England, descended mostly from English stock, are genetically distinguishable from those in New York, descended mostly from Dutch stock.

By the Middle Ages, Europeans had settled on the cat as their rodent catcher; but it was no more than that. Cats are constantly portrayed in medieval manuscripts and carvings. Most often, they are playing with or clutching mice, although sometimes they nurse or carry kittens. A cat holds a mouse in her mouth on a misericord in Winchester Cathedral; a gray tabby sits up batting a mouse between her paws on a margin of the Luttrell Psalter (c. 1330). The drawing is anatomically awkward, but the cat's pose has been precisely observed. Typically, these representations

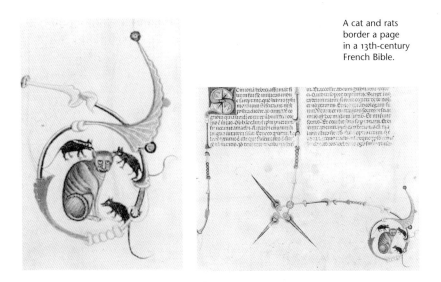

simply show cats as a familiar part of everyday life; but occasionally there are suggestions of their traditional association with witches. An old woman spins under the eyes of two grotesque cats on a stall in the Minster church on the Isle of Thanet, and one rides a cat on a misericord in Winchester Cathedral.

According to King Hywel Dda's codification of Welsh law early in the tenth century, a cat mature enough to catch mice was valued at four pence, the same as a peasant's cur. The cat was worth less if it was immature, had defective sight or hearing, or was addicted to going out caterwauling.[12] The expression 'to let the cat out of the bag' (traceable to the sixteenth century) shows how limited was a cat's value even in utilitarian terms. A gullible person who was foolish enough to buy 'a pig in a poke' (bag) – that is, sight unseen – might find when he opened it that he had nothing but a cat.

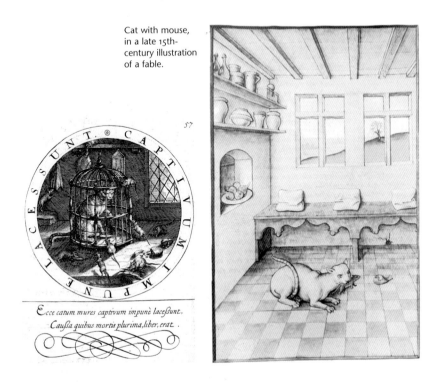

Cat with mouse, in a late 15th-century illustration of a fable.

Ecce catum mures captivum impunè laceßunt.
Cauſa quibus mortis plurima, liber, erat .

In this plate from an emblem book of 1635, the cat is rightly caged because it represents a wicked magistrate; the accompanying moral likens a cat who eats more cheese than the mice to a corrupt magistrate who steals more from society than the thieves he sends to prison.

Because the cat was defined as a rodent killer, and because it hunts on its own, it was and still is seen as more predatory than the dog. Hounds and terriers were bred for killing prey and are still enthusiastic about chasing small animals, but they are rarely presented as ruthless and bloodthirsty. The fact that the cat hunts for itself rather than for human gratification supports the prevailing idea that it selfishly pursues its own interests, in contrast to the dog, who serves and supports man. In Buddhist folklore, a rat was sent for medicine to cure the Buddha when he was mortally ill, but it could not fulfil its mission because a cat seized and ate it on its way. In another version, the cat was the

28

A single line conveys the ferocity of a feline hunter in this illustration, 'A Cat and a Cock', by Alexander Calder for a 1931 edition of the *Fables of Aesop*.

The proverbial hostility of cats and dogs, as depicted in a late 15th-century French manuscript of *Proverbes en Rimes*.

only animal not overwhelmed with awe when the Buddha was passing into Nirvana: it was too intent on eyeing the rat.[13]

Because the cat sneaks up on its prey rather than forthrightly rushing it down like a dog, humans have called it sly and underhanded, even hypocritical. Only five Aesopian fables feature cats, and two of them turn on their predatory guile. In number 94, having killed most of the mice in a house, the cat tries to lure out the rest by shamming death, and in number 95, he tries to catch the sick hens on a farm by disguising himself as a doctor. In a famous fable in the Indian compilation *Pancatantra*, a partridge and a hare go to consult a neighbouring cat, who lives as a hermit and maintains the highest reputation for holiness and compassion. As they approach, the cat recites edifying sayings about the all-importance of righteousness and the evil of injuring any creature, especially a harmless one. Their trust in him confirmed, the small animals beg him to settle a dispute between them, but the cat tells them he is old and deaf and they must come closer so he can be sure he understands them fully and

Two small petitioners approach a cat whose sanctified appearance conceals his predatory intentions. The scene is an illustration by Grandville to La Fontaine's version (1838) of the ancient Hindu fable of the 'Devout Cat'.

thus can arrive at the right judgement. So they come right up to him, when of course the cat promptly pounces and kills them.[14] This story is told all over India and is immortalized in a famous bas relief at Mahabalipuram in southern India, where the cat stands up on his hind legs with arms extended toward heaven, in a parody of the posture of a pious ascetic.

The sweet, peaceful demeanour of a cat in repose, together with its keenly predatory nature, have made it an emblem of hypocrisy in the West as well. In a widespread folk tale recorded by the Brothers Grimm, 'The Cat and Mouse in Partnership', a cat professes love and friendship so persuasively to a mouse that she agrees to set up housekeeping together. At the cat's suggestion, they buy a large pot of fat to sustain them when winter comes and store it in the church. One day the cat longs for some fat, so she tells the mouse she must go away on family business; she goes straight to the church, eats off the top of the fat, and strolls around town for the rest of the day. She repeats this manoeuvre twice, finishing the fat on her third excursion. When winter sets in and there is no food to be found, the mouse

Illustration by H. J. Ford to the fairy story 'The Cat and the Mouse in Partnership' (1894).

suggests that they go and enjoy their fat. Of course, she finds the pot empty; and when she realizes what has happened and scolds the cat, the cat quiets her by eating her up.[15]

Cats incur further charges of moral turpitude because, instead of immediately killing their prey and wolfing it down, they may prefer to defer eating and play with their catch. Edmund Burke made brilliant use of the contrast between apparent feline blandness and actual feline ruthlessness in his *Letter to a Noble Lord* (1795): ideologues who think nothing of sacrificing humanity in pursuit of their utopian experiments resemble 'the grave, demure, insidious, spring-nailed, velvet-pawed, green-eyed philosophers' who play dispassionately with the mice they have caught.[16] Accordingly, catty means slyly spiteful and feline connotes stealth. To play cat and mouse with is to toy with a victim in one's power, and the children's game 'Puss in the Corner' involves surrounding and teasing one of the players by offering and withdrawing opportunities to escape.

On the other hand, the cat's guile may be justified as the necessary resource of a small predator. The beast epic *Reynard the Fox* (written down in 1250) portrays a ruthless world in which the large predators represent the ruling class and the small ones the peasants. Sympathy is directed not to the prey animals, but toward the relatively weak predators who must survive by their wits. Tybert the Cat is second in cunning only to Reynard the Fox himself. Cats and foxes are similarly associated in Japanese folklore, although the cat is generally presented more sympathetically than the fox.

Only in the nineteenth century, when love and appreciation of cats first became widespread, did people begin to admire feline guile and hunting ability without qualification. Charles Henry Ross compiled *The Book of Cats: Feline Facts and Fancies, Legendary, Lyrical, Medical, Mirthful and Miscellaneous* (1868), in

Tybert the cat castrates a village priest in a 15th-century woodcut illustrating *The History of Reynard the Fox.*

which he celebrated cats such as a clever tom in Callander who stole a bit of beef to lure a rat out of his hole. St George Mivart, a Darwinian zoologist, used the unlikely venue of a dissection manual to exalt the cat as a superb example of the survival of the fittest. He became so enthusiastic about the functional design of the cat family that he promoted them to the position of the highest mammals after man: the Carnivora are the highest order of mammals because they are at the top of the food chain, and the Felidae, house cats included, are the best adapted carnivores.

James White's story 'The Conspirators' (1954) reflects not only the modern affection for cats but the twentieth-century readiness to accept their natural predacity. The hero, Felix, fulfils the traditional role of ship's cat, although he travels on a space ship. It has passed through an atmosphere that heightens intelligence, acting first on the smaller animals. Felix's mental and moral intelligence has been greatly enhanced, although he is surpassed by the laboratory mice on board, and the humans have not yet improved. The enlightened mice have discovered what happens to laboratory animals and conspire to get off the ship, and they must depend on the cat to help them because only he can move about freely without causing suspicion. His mind has enlarged to the point that he no longer sees the mice simply as prey, although he cannot yet consistently see them as intelligent comrades, and the mice retain suspicions of him. Felix, with his intellectual challenges and moral conflict, has come a very long way from the single-minded hunters of *Aesop's Fables*.[17]

Regardless of the human assumption that they were nothing more than useful little hunters, cats succeeded in moving into people's homes. Numerous proverbs and folk tales represent the dog as being left outside, while the cat enjoys a warm spot in

Pub sign for the Cat & Fiddle in Bodmin, Cornwall.

the kitchen. Geoffrey Chaucer's self-indulgent friar in 'The Summoner's Tale' (*c.* 1390) has to dislodge the cat before appropriating the most comfortable seat in the house. Unlike the classical compilers, Bartholomew Anglicus, author of the widely read encyclopedia *De Proprietatibus rerum*, had obviously observed cats around the house. In youth a cat 'is swift, pliant, and merry', leaps and rushes at everything that moves, and plays with straws; in age he 'is a right heavy beast . . . and full sleepy, and lieth slyly in wait for mice'. Like most medieval writers on the natural world, however, Bartholomew could not resist adding a fanciful detail that lent itself to moral edification: a cat that normally parades around the neighbourhood proud of its

A cat is shown comfortably indoors by Cristoforo Rustici (1560–1640) in 'The Month of January'.

appearance can be kept at home by singeing its fur. While cats are indeed obsessively preoccupied with the condition of their coat, the reference to pride suggests a human application, analogous to Aristotle's imputation of lechery to female cats. Preaching friars made the most of these associations by constantly applying them to vain women. Nicholas Bozon sadistically elaborated: just as a cat can be made to stay at home by shortening her tail, cutting her ears and singeing her fur, women can be kept there by shortening the trains of their dresses, disarranging their headdresses and staining their clothes.[18]

Since cats were kept solely for their utility in keeping down the rodent population, no one noticed their beauty, charm, or capacity for companionship. They rarely appear in literature, and then only to furnish stock comparisons such as likening a cruel mistress to a cat playing with a mouse. Even William Shakespeare's imagination was not inspired by the cat. Like his mundane Shylock, he saw it as no more than a 'harmless necessary' animal. His Benedick jokes about the practice of hanging up a cat in a leather bag to shoot at it; his Lysander calls Hermia a cat for showing the cat's claws and aggressive sexuality; his Tarquin hears Lucrece's prayers like a cat dallying with the mouse panting under his paw; his Lady Macbeth goads her husband with the proverb about the cat who wants to eat fish but not to wet its feet.[19]

Visual artists recognized the decorative value of cats long before writers noticed their charm. Renaissance painters included cats when they placed religious events in contemporary settings, especially when the Biblical scenes involved eating. Tintoretto included a cat in three of his six versions of the Last Supper, in his *Christ at Emmaus* and in *Belshazzar's Feast*. In one *Last Supper* (1592–4), a bold, sturdy cat occupies the exact centre of the foreground, in front of the table where Christ sits with the Apostles. It stands on its hind legs to investigate what is inside the basket from which a maid is taking food, while a barely visible dog watches wistfully from under the table. In a *Supper at Emmaus* by Philippe de Champaigne (1602–74), a cat in the centre foreground is actively engaged in snagging leftovers from a plate, while a servant pushes it away. This lifelike practical conflict contrasts strikingly with the stiffly painted figures absorbed in edifying conversation above the table. The cat could not be less interested in the resurrected Jesus, but it is too attractively painted, with its soft silver tabby fur and its sweet expression, to evoke moral condemnation.

These animals were probably included to make a spiritual event more accessible by domesticating it. Sometimes, however, the cat's conspicuous lack of interest in human activities does

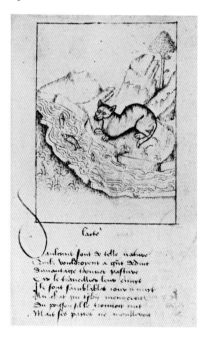

Illustration of the proverb that cats long to eat fish but do not want to wet their feet, from a late 15th-century French manuscript of *Proverbes en Rimes*.

In a painting by the Master of the Life of St Joseph, c. 1500, a baleful cat with human eyes sits by Pharaoh's butler, who is in the act of making a false promise to Joseph.

take on moral implications. A cat that pointedly dissociates itself from a sacred scene – like the sullen cat with ears laid back that crouches on a stool at the edge of Jacopo Bassano's *Last Supper* (1546–8) – may seem to be alien, even hostile, to holy things. In Domenico Ghirlandaio's *Last Supper* (1481), Judas sits alone on one side of the table, his isolation emphasized by a cat sitting on the floor beside him and staring directly at the viewer, while Judas pretends to take part in the social interaction. The cat in the center of Lorenzo Lotto's *Annunciation* (c. 1527) is actively hostile: it rushes, distraught, away from the angel who announces to Mary that she will bear the Son of God and thus make possible the divine plan for the salvation of humanity. Several pictures of the

Holy Family include cats that prowl or sleep or stalk birds while all the humans in the scene are worshipping Jesus. In Giulio Romano's *Madonna of the Cat*, Mary gazes lovingly at baby Jesus, who extends his arms toward an adoring John the Baptist; meanwhile, an avidly greedy cat schemes to steal food from a plate on the floor. When the cat is stalking a goldfinch, as it does in Federico Barocci's *Madonna with a Cat* (*c*. 1574), it is symbolically jeopardizing the divine scheme for the salvation of humanity; for birds represent the soul and the goldfinch, because its taste for

While the Virgin, St Anne and John the Baptist adore the infant Jesus, a sinister cat glares belligerently, its golden eyes fixed on a plate of food, in Giulio Romano's *Madonna of the Cat, c.* 1523, oil on panel.

thistles suggests the crown of thorns, introduces an added reference to Christ's redeeming passion. Three centuries later, William Holman Hunt took up the same symbolism in his *Awakening of Conscience* (1853). A young kept woman has just resolved to reform and starts out of her lover's lap. Under the table, a wicked-looking tabby cat looks up with fiery orange eyes, so unpleasantly startled by her moral transformation that it has released the bird it has caught. Like the cats in Renaissance Holy Family pictures, it is trying to catch a bird, symbolic of the soul, but is frustrated by divine grace. C. S. Lewis drew on this traditional symbolism in *The Last Battle* (the last chronicle of Narnia, 1956), where the cold irreverent tomcat Ginger leads in the scheme to overthrow the divine order, incarnated in the noble lion Aslan.

In secular works, cats are also typically associated with food, which they are usually stealing. Guiseppe Recco's *Cat Stealing Fish* looks up with a defiant snarl when it is disturbed raiding a pile of fish. Behind a luxuriously set table in Alexandre-François Desportes' *Still-life with a Cat* (*c.* 1661–73), we see the head and paw of a cat that has just hooked an oyster. With its big eyes focused on its catch, its ears pricked forward and its mouth set in naughty resolution, the cat is vividly intent on carrying off its prey before any human might interfere. In a companion piece, *Still-life with a Dog*, a spaniel sniffs wistfully at a ham on a table. Frans Snyders portrayed a mother cat plundering a heap of dead game with her family: she pulls at a peacock, one kitten has seized a little bird and two others are about to jump for one apiece. They are unreconstructed wild hunters, in contrast to the dog that sleeps peacefully in the foreground. Cats often add to the atmosphere of animal indulgence and impropriety in Dutch genre scenes of revelry in taverns. But in *The King Drinks* (*c.* 1640–45), Jacob Jordaens made the cat's aloofness a positive

quality. The sour, baleful tomcat crouching in the foreground pointedly isolates himself from a coarse and jolly Epiphany revel full of drinking and vomiting, while a dog watches eagerly, apparently longing for a drink.

Alexandre-François Desportes, *Still-life with a Cat*, late 17th century, oil on canvas.

At best cats were considered harmless and necessary; at worst, they were common animals of negligible monetary value and were therefore handy victims for casual sadism. They were easily obtainable at no cost and are satisfyingly demonstrative when subjected to pain. They were stuffed into an effigy of the Pope at Queen Elizabeth's coronation procession, providing vivid sound effects when it was burned. They were slowly burned on St John's Eve at the Place de Grève in Paris, after which the people

Illustration by Wenceslaus Hollar of a fable in which a deputation of mice try to propitiate the cat; after pretending to agree to a peace treaty, he routs and kills them.

collected their ashes as good luck charms. This celebration lasted until 1648, when Louis XIV presided. When the victorious Puritan rebels in England wanted to demonstrate their contempt for Anglican churches, they hunted a cat with hounds through Lichfield Cathedral every day (1643) and roasted a cat on a spit in

Ely Cathedral (1638). The official recorders of these events were shocked by the vandalism and profanation, not the cruelty.[20]

Cruelty to animals was generally accepted in the Early Modern period because it was not condemned by any Christian church. Thomas Aquinas argued in his *Summa Theologica* that we have no obligation to extend charity to 'irrational animals' that lack free will, cannot participate in a society 'regulated by reason' and cannot attain everlasting life. Moreover, by giving man dominion over the other animals, God gave us permission to treat them any way we like. René Descartes reinforced this position in the seventeenth century by locating consciousness and feelings, as well as free will, in the rational soul: since only humans have a soul, animals cannot feel pain or emotion any more than a machine can; logically, then, what would be manifestations of pain in humans are merely meaningless, automatic movements in other animals.[21]

Muhammad had a more enlightened attitude: he taught that Allah requires kindness not only to people but to all his creatures. Although he forbade all cruelty to animals, such as branding a donkey on a sensitive spot or organizing animal fights, he had a particular fondness for cats. There is a widely accepted tradition that one day Muhammad's cat was sleeping on his cloak when he was called to prayers; he took off his cloak rather than disturb the animal. He was so shocked by a woman who had kept her cat locked up until it slowly died, refusing either to feed it or allow it to go out and forage for itself, that he repeatedly told how he had seen her in a vision of Hell, being lacerated by a cat. While dogs were considered unclean in the Arab world, a cat could eat from a human's dish of food or drink the water for ablutions without polluting them. The cat 'is not unclean', Muhammad said; 'it is one of those . . . who go round among you'. That is, cats had the run of the house, while dogs (only used for working or hunting) were kept outside. A close companion of Muhammad was called 'Abu Huraira', Father of Cats, because of his particular attachment to them. One day, it is said, the Prophet was threatened by a snake and Abu Huraira's cat killed the snake just in time. In return, Muhammad stroked her back, ensuring that cats never fall on their backs, and ran his fingers over her head, leaving the four stripes still to be found on the forehead of a tabby cat.

In the Moslem world, it was cats, rather than dogs, that were pampered, kissed and allowed to sleep in their owners' beds. The ninth-century poet Ibn al-Mu'tazz wrote an epitaph on his cat, who was 'like a son' to him, but unfortunately strayed into a neighbour's pigeon-house and was executed. A thirteenth-century sultan endowed a 'cats' garden' to provide for the cats of Cairo, and people bring food there to this day.[22]

In the West, moral concern for animals became general only in the eighteenth century, when the religious law that excluded beasts from moral consideration gave way to a sentimental morality that emphasized good feeling over moral law and focused on the lower animals' capacity for feeling rather than their lack of human reason. A systematic opposition to cruelty toward animals began to take shape, powered by a new emphasis on kindness toward the helpless and dependent. Alexander Pope taught in the *Essay on Man* (1733–4) that we share the creation with animals, and since the barrier between us and them is so very thin, we are not entitled to abuse or exploit them. When he condemned cruelty to animals, he singled out cats because they were particularly victimized: they 'have the misfortune, for no manner of reason, to be treated as common enemies wherever found. The conceit that a cat has nine lives has cost at least nine lives in ten of the whole race of them: scarce a boy in the streets but has in this point outdone Hercules himself, who was famous for killing a monster that had but three lives.'[23]

Although keeping cats as pets was becoming normal in the eighteenth century, most people still saw them as no more than humble domestic animals, kept for use and deserving humane treatment only because they were sentient. Edward Moore's fable 'The Farmer, the Spaniel, and the Cat' represents a farmer sharing his dinner with his spaniel as a matter of course. When his cat 'humbly craved a servant's share' and the dog objected to her getting any, she meekly conceded his superior merit, but pointed out that she contributed 'to the good of man' insofar as her nature allowed; that is, by killing rats and mice. On the basis of this plea, the farmer threw her a morsel.[24]

Because the cat was identified with the essential but humdrum function of rodent-catching it was not thought of as a luxury animal. The thirteenth-century *Ancrene Riwle*, an austere guidebook for young women dedicated to the religious life, allowed them to keep no animal except a cat. After William Hogarth's Moll

In one of a series of engravings by William Hogarth, *The Harlot's Progress* (1732), the cat indicates both Moll's profession and her decline in financial status.

Playful kittens in a typically sentimental 19th-century oil painting by Louis-Eugène Lambert, *Cadeau à Mme Lambert*.

Hackabout is thrown out by her rich keeper and declines into a common prostitute, she shares her squalid room with a cat (Plate 3 of *The Harlot's Progress*, 1732). A worried looking cat nurses her kittens in the wretched garret occupied by the family of Hogarth's *Distressed Poet* (1737). In China, the arrival of a strange cat in a house was supposed to portend poverty, because the cat foresaw that the house would soon fall into dilapidation and therefore be overrun with mice.

Cats were widely appreciated as pets in the nineteenth century, but they did not contribute to their owner's prestige like dogs or horses. In 1881 Mivart called the cat 'the inmate of a

Even in the cat-loving 19th century, there were alternative views. Although Edwin Landseer fondly sentimentalized most animals, his painting *The Cat's Paw* (c. 1824), in which a monkey forces a cat to pull his chestnuts out of the fire, is positively sadistic.

multitude of humble homes where the dog has no place'. Thorstein Veblen, who scorned dogs as striking examples of conspicuous consumption, approvingly pointed out that the cat is useless as a status symbol: she can be acquired for little or nothing, can be supported cheaply and might even 'serve a useful purpose'; nor does she look up to her owner. More conventional people dismissed cats as worthless because their owners were so often poor people. Noblemen's gamekeepers had no scruples about killing cats as threats to game and displaying their stuffed bodies, along with those of hawks, owls and weasels. Even the Royal Society for the Prevention of Cruelty to Animals initially neglected to include a cat among the domestic animals pictured on its Queen's Medal for Kindness. Queen Victoria insisted that one be placed in the foreground, explaining that the royal family should do something to change public aversion to and contempt for cats, 'which were generally misunderstood and grossly ill-treated'.[25]

2 The Magic of Cats, Evil and Good

Even when cats were typically perceived as common and insignificant though useful, there has always been something about them that distinguishes them from ordinary domesticated animals. They move silently, unpredictably and with perfect precision – so inconspicuously as to suggest that they can magically appear and disappear. They see in near darkness and hear sounds inaudible to humans, even when they appear to be napping. They can anticipate earthquakes and severe electrical storms (presumably through natural sensitivity to minute vibrations or to an increase in static electricity). Indeed, their senses are so superior to our own that we imagine that they have preternatural knowledge, even the ability to predict the future. (We do not marvel at the dog's equally remarkable senses, because we see it as our subordinate ally; instead, we take them for granted as a practical means to augment our own.) Cats have a habit of looking at us steadily without showing any sign of emotional engagement. The cat's dispassionate, wide-eyed gaze, unusually direct for an animal, arouses suspicions that it is challenging us or relentlessly searching into our inner selves. These natural qualities can readily be interpreted as evidence of uncanny abilities, which may be perceived as divine or demonic.

Although cats live closer to humans than any other animals except dogs, they do not share the dog's exuberant emotional

The forthright gaze of the cat: a 19th-century Russian folk print or *loubok*, 'The Cat Alabrys'.

expressiveness or its eagerness to please, to be loved, to engage in fellowship with people. Self-contained, independent, quietly pursuing their own agenda, they seem to live in a world of their own, inaccessible to humans. In the words that Angela Carter playfully puts into the mouth of Puss in Boots, in her interpretation of the tale, cats always wear 'small, cool, quiet Mona Lisa smiles . . . So all cats have a politician's air; we smile and smile and so they think we're villains.'[1] Humans can easily imagine the cat listening in on the family conversation for some sinister purpose of its own, as it does in the Irish folktale 'Owney and Owney-Na-Peak'.

We think of cats as lower animals, and yet they live in our households without acknowledging any inferiority. In the medieval and early modern periods, when a hierarchical order in society and nature was assumed to be right and necessary, their disregard for human wishes and expectations was unpleasantly disconcerting. Moreover, because the natural dominion of man was ordained by providence, their refusal to recognize it demonstrated antagonism to God as well as man. Therefore, it seemed likely that their secret nocturnal world was presided over by the Prince of Darkness.

From the Middle Ages through the early modern period, the cat's seemingly supernatural abilities, together with its cool detachment from human concerns, laid it open to suspicion. This provided any rationalization that might be needed for rituals such as slowly burning cats to death on St John's Eve, 23 June, in order to expel evil from the Christian community and protect the growing crops by driving away evil spirits. Because of their supposed congeniality with Satan, cats were used to extract concessions from him. A coven of witches in North Berwick, who confessed to raising a storm in order to wreck the ship on which King James VI was bringing his queen from Denmark in 1590, explained that they achieved their purpose by christening a cat, binding pieces of a dead man to each part of it, and throwing it into the sea. In the hideous Taigheirm ritual of Scotland, a person striving to obtain the second sight would slowly roast cats as a sacrifice to the infernal powers. If the human perpetrator and his succession of victims could hold out for four solid days, the spirits from hell would appear in the form of black cats and grant his wish. Similar beliefs persisted among uneducated people as late as the nineteenth century, as the heroine of Elizabeth Gaskell's *North and South* (1855) is appalled to discover. When she returns to her father's rural parish, an old peasant woman complains that Betty Barnes has stolen her cat and roasted it alive as a magical spell to avert her husband's anger, on the assumption that the cries of a cat in agony would compel the powers of darkness to fulfill her wishes. The woman does not doubt the efficacy of the spell, nor would she have been distressed by the cruelty had the victim not been her own cat.[2]

A cat might be a demon himself. A fisherman in Connemara always brought in plenty of fish, but every night a great black cat would come in and eat the best ones before they could be got to market. One night he came in when the fisherman's wife was there, looked over the fish that was laid out on the tables, and warned her not to disturb him or make a fuss. Then he jumped up and started to devour the fish, growling at the woman when she approached. She tried to drive him off with a blow that should have broken his back, but he only grinned at her and went on tearing at the fish. But when she got a bottle of holy water and threw some on him, his body burned to a cinder and disappeared.[3]

Cats were more often accused of allying themselves with human agents of Satan, providing alternative forms for witches and assisting them as familiars. However, although animals were prominent in witchcraft superstitions because of their importance in pagan worship, the animals involved were not necessarily cats. Women accused of witchcraft in the sixteenth and seventeenth centuries were supposed to turn themselves into hares as often as cats, and their familiars might be mongrel dogs, mice or even toads. It was only in later centuries, when witchcraft became a picturesque theme for fantasy and cats were perceived as attractively exotic and mysterious, that they became the featured animal.

Nevertheless, cats did frequently appear in the witch trials. Their love of physical intimacy with those they like and their ability to appear and disappear without warning would have particularly suited them to be familiars. Fond owners would

In a 1909 cover for *Harper's Weekly*, witch and familiar have been trivialized into a pretty girl and a cute kitten.

A 20th-century postcard reduces the Salem witch-craft panic to a joke.

naturally cuddle, pamper or talk to their cats; and this behaviour automatically laid them open to a charge of witchcraft. Elizabeth Francis, a farmer's wife condemned in Essex in 1566, had learned witchcraft from her grandmother, who had given her a white spotted cat, imprudently named Sathan, and instructed her to give him her blood, feed him on bread and milk, and keep him in a basket. He spoke to her 'in a strange hollow voice', which she learned to understand. She asked the cat to make her rich and get her a husband, rewarding him with drops of her blood, which she produced by pricking herself in various places that left lasting red spots. On the cat's advice, she tried to get Andrew Byles to marry her by letting him seduce her; when he refused, she got Sathan to destroy his goods and then kill him. Afterwards, Sathan did get her a husband; but she became unhappy with him and got the cat to kill their child and inflict lameness on the man. Finally she gave Sathan to Mother Agnes Waterhouse in exchange for a cake, and he obliged his new owner by killing a cow and three geese belonging to her neighbours.[4]

Jean Bodin, a noted witch-hunter, relates that in 1561 at Vernon in France, witches and wizards used to assemble at night in an old castle in the shape of cats. Some bold investigators went to watch them; one was killed and the others badly clawed. However, they managed to wound several of the cats, and the next day some of the suspected humans appeared with similar wounds. Elizabeth Morse, accused as a witch in Massachusetts in 1679–80, attacked a neighbour in the form of a strange 'white thing like a cat'; he managed to smash it against a fence, and that very night, he learned, Goodwife Morse had been treated by a doctor for a wounded head. The same 'great white cat' assaulted another witness by climbing on his chest, seizing his neckcloth and coat, and coming 'between [his] legs, so that [he] could not well go forward' – normal feline behaviour, of course, though made sinister by human preconceptions.[5]

In the folktale 'The Haunted Mill', a miller could not keep an apprentice because of the horrible nightly disturbances in his mill; finally a young man volunteered to spend the night there with his axe and his prayer book. On the stroke of twelve, an old and a young gray cat came in and sat down, meowing to each other and clearly annoyed to find a wide-awake armed man. They snatched at the axe and book, but he was too quick for them. At 1 a.m. the younger cat batted at the candle to put it out, but the young man managed to prevent her by striking off her right paw with the axe. The next day, he saw that what he had was not a paw, but a hand. The miller's wife did not want to appear; when she did, they saw why – her right hand was missing.[6]

Shape-shifting between women and cats (as well as foxes) is also a common theme in Japanese folklore. The evil creatures in the Japanese stories are not women taking the form of cats, but demon cats taking the form of women, typically seductive ones. They were human size, with huge glaring eyes and teeth that they fixed in their victim's neck. In a culture where cats were preferably bob-tailed, they often had a long double tail. 'The Vampire Cat of Nabeshima' tells how one night a huge cat entered the bedroom of O Toyo, favourite lady of the prince of Hizen, throttled her, buried her corpse, and assumed her form. (Felines kill large prey animals by choking off their breath with a bite to the throat.) The prince, who knew nothing of this, continued to love the false O Toyo. Night by night his strength failed until he became dangerously ill, and physicians could not help him. Since he suffered most during the night and was troubled by horrible dreams, a hundred of his retainers were set to keep watch while he slept; but just before ten o'clock, they were all overcome with sleep. Then the false O Toyo glided in to suck

Illustration to a well-known Japanese folk tale, *The Vampire Cat of Nabeshima*, 19th-century woodblock print. The huge demon-cat throttling a lady has the characteristic double tail.

his neck until sunrise. Finally a young soldier, convinced the prince was bewitched, came to watch by him. He managed to avoid falling asleep by twisting his dagger in his thigh, and so he saw a beautiful woman approaching the prince. By staring fixedly at her, he prevented her from exerting her witchcraft, and she had to retire. The same thing happened the next night. Now sure of the truth, the soldier went to the false O Toyo's room to kill her. She turned back into a cat, sprang onto the roof, and escaped to harass the local people. Ultimately, the prince organized a hunt and killed her.[7]

These demon-cat stories took particular hold on people's imaginations because many of them, such as 'The Cat-Witch of Okabe', were enacted on the stage. This witch was a cat who appeared in the form of an old woman and haunted and terrified the young virgins who served at the local sanctuary. In Utagawa Kuniyoshi's portrayal of a kabuki performance of about 1835, a malevolent woman with large cat's ears and furry clawed paws kneels in the centre, with a huge, glaring cat crouched behind her and a samurai on each side attempting to strike her down. By each of the samurai is a cat dancing on its hind legs with a cloth bound around its head, alluding to the folk belief that if a napkin is missing, the cat must have stolen it to put on its head and join in a dance of the cats, who howl at the top of their voices, 'Neko ja! We are cats!' Typically they do this in the main hall of a temple or some other place that should be kept quiet.[8]

This maniacal dance was witnessed by a samurai when he took shelter for the night in a lonely mountain temple, only what the cats were yelling was 'Tell it not to Shippeitaro'. The next day he found out at the nearest village that every year these cats forced the peasants to shut their fairest maiden into a cage and take her to the temple to be devoured by the spirit of the mountain. Wanting to help, the samurai asked them who or what was Shippeitaro. They told him it was a brave and fine dog belonging to their head man; the samurai borrowed the dog, put him in the cage prepared for the girl, and had it carried to

Utagawa Kuniyoshi, *The Cat-Witch of Okabe*, c. 1835, woodblock print. Two samurai are attempting to strike down the malevolent old witch, who has a cat's ears and paws; a giant cat looms behind her, and two ordinary ones dance in fiendish glee.

the temple. At midnight the phantom cats reappeared, along with a monstrously huge and ferocious tomcat, who sprang to the cage with screams of delight and, after sufficiently taunting his supposed victim, opened the door. But it was Shippeitaro who rushed out and seized hold of the tomcat, so that the samurai could dispatch him with his sword. Then the dog killed all the other cats, and the village was freed from their oppression.[9]

The thought of large gatherings of cats aroused unease in Europe as well. People said that the neighbourhood cats held secret meetings that humans had better not intrude on. Sometimes the mischief could be prevented by cutting off the ends of their tails, in the same way that Japanese docked the

A cat leads a temperance rally in M. Brière's drawing, *Assembly of Cats* (1912).

58

tails of long-tailed kittens in order to deprive them of the sinister powers conferred by these organs. A Breton story tells how the local cats would assemble by moonlight on certain days near the Fairy Rocks and the Standing Stones. Sensible people stayed well away from this place, but Jean Foucault, returning home drunk and happily singing, stumbled into the assembly. His voice stuck in his throat as he saw the cats arch their backs, swell their tails, and stare at him with glowing eyes. When the biggest of all rushed at him, he shut his eyes and recited his act of contrition, for he expected to be torn in pieces. But instead of claws, he felt the soft, warm fur of a cat's back rubbing along his legs and heard joyful purring; it turned out to be his own cat, who escorted him through the assembly, telling the others to let him pass. The story is based on the traditional suspicion that cats have supernatural powers that they are likely to use against humans, but here it has been modified by the modern recognition that they can be friendly companions.

In an Irish tale, 'Owney and Owney-Na-Peak', the hero makes his fortune when he wanders past the graveyard one night and happens on a great meeting of the local cats, including his own. He overhears from them the secret of how to cure the king's blindness. As he is repeating it to his cousin, he notices that his cat is listening, so he takes care to wait until she leaves the room and to close the door after her. Even in the nineteenth century, Gascon peasants affirmed that cats were regularly paid by the devil to keep watch, although they could not say what the cats' wages might be or what they did with them: 'Fools take no precautions about cats, but discreet people mistrust them. Many of these beasts have formed a contract with the devil, who pays them to keep watch all night, and be sentinels, when the evil spirits assemble.' Cats sleep all day, or pretend to do so, because 'they are tired from patrolling all night . . . with such good sentinels, evil spirits always get warning to disappear in time.' It is particularly imprudent to become familiar with one's cat, for cats have a natural inclination to assume equality with humans and will exact vengeance if they do not get privileges they have been led to expect. A woman in a French story loved her cat so much that she let him eat at the table with her. When she excluded him one day because she had company, he throttled her during the night. Another cat took the same revenge when his mistress punished him for dressing up in human clothes while she was at church.[10]

Even scientific writers might endow cats with malignant powers that bordered on the supernatural. These authors did have two actual conditions to build on. One was ailurophobia, an irrational fear of cats, triggered by their sudden unpredictable movements and their habit of sitting and staring with two big eyes. This is far from the most common animal phobia, but it has attracted disproportionate attention; and it is true that cats can cause panic attacks, even fainting, in some people. The other condition is the much more common allergy to cats (or, more specifically, to the dander resulting from cat saliva when they lick their fur), which affects 5 to 10 per cent of the population of the United States. This can produce not only watering of the nose and eyes, but asthma leading to a terrifying stoppage of breath. Ambroise Paré, a distinguished physician, heightened these small effects to make the cat into a truly dangerous animal. He wrote in his treatise *Of Poisons* (c. 1575) that its stare can cause a susceptible person to fall unconscious, and proceeded to a long list of imaginary examples of 'malicious virulency' in the cat. He claimed that its brain, hair and breath are poisonous to humans and that sleeping with one causes tuberculosis.[11]

Edward Topsell elaborated on Paré's list in his *History of Four-Footed Beasts and Serpents and Insects* (1607), which purported to

be a natural history. People who sleep with cats fall into consumption because a cat's breath destroys the lungs. Its flesh is poisonous, its 'venomous teeth' inflict a deadly bite, and swallowing its hair unawares causes suffocation. Like Paré, he blames cats for the ailurophobes' reaction to them: cats can 'poison a man with very looking upon him', since some men have a natural abhorrence of cats that causes them to 'fall into passions, frettings, sweating, pulling off their hats, and trembling fearfully'. Cats' expressive vocalizations suggest that they have the power of speech, and even that they 'have a peculiar intelligible language among themselves'. The cat uses her rough tongue to lick human flesh so vigorously that she draws blood, and when human blood mixes with her spittle, she runs mad. At night her eyes 'can hardly be endured, for their flaming aspect'. (The last two lurid charges were lifted from the Roman Pliny, who had applied them, with almost equal ludicrousness, to lions and leopards.) This indictment was supposed to have a moral purpose: to warn people against consorting with cats, not only because affection for animals without immortal souls was impious, but because it is intrinsically imprudent. Some monks who caressed the monastery cat fell sick, Topsell relates, because the cat had picked up poison from playing with a serpent and, unhurt herself, transmitted it to the men. Finally, 'the familiars of Witches do most commonly appear in the shape of Cats, which is an argument that this beast is dangerous to soul and body'.[12]

By 1711, when Joseph Addison wrote a *Spectator* essay to ridicule belief in witchcraft, it was dismissed it as a medieval superstition by all educated people and, concurrently, the particular connection between witches and cats was firmly established. Credulous neighbours suspect poor old Moll White of witchcraft because she is intimate with a tabby cat, who is reputed to be her familiar and 'to have spoken twice or thrice in her life, and to have played several Pranks above the Capacity of an ordinary Cat'.[13]

Both witches and cats were romanticized in the nineteenth century. The many people who found witchcraft titillating and also liked cats saw feline detachment, private nocturnal ways and unpredictability as intriguing rather than hostile, and imagined that these qualities would be even more fascinating if they came from the devil. Thus Walter Scott, who loved all his pets and particularly pampered his cats, remarked: 'Ah! Cats are a mysterious kind of folk. There is more passing in their minds than we are aware of. It comes no doubt from their being too familiar with warlocks and witches.' Edgar Allan Poe praised his clever black cat as 'one of the most remarkable black cats in the world – and this is saying much; for it will be remembered that black cats are all of them witches'.[14]

For the many nineteenth-century French artists who gloried in their alienation from the respectable bourgeoisie, cats with their traditional demonic associations were a perfect symbol for the artist's rejection of conventional standards and assumptions. These artists saw a parallel between the cat's supposed occult knowledge and their own superior perceptiveness, between its supposed attraction to evil and their own impulse to shock the bourgeois. A taste for what is demonic and forbidden, in cat as in artist, indicated superiority because it proved one's ability to see through the obtuse complacency of ordinary people. The cat's beauty, detachment and indifference to morality made it congenial to artists who rejected moralizing to pursue art for art's sake. The white cat that amuses itself in the centre foreground of Gustave Courbet's *The Artist's Studio* (1855), totally unconcerned with the activities of everyone else in the crowded scene, is an emblem of the artist's own disregard for convention and the artistic establishment.

Théophile Gautier's preface to the posthumous edition of the poems of his friend Charles-Pierre Baudelaire lists the diverse charms they found in the cat: both its beauty and tactful companionship (appreciated by modern writers of all schools) and its familiarity with sinister powers and occult knowledge, derived from ancestors that were worshipped by the wise Egyptians. Recent archaeological investigations had revived knowledge of the cat's high place in ancient Egypt, which was seized on and exaggerated by contemporary ailurophiles. Cats' 'favourite attitude is the extended pose of the sphinxes, which seem to have passed their secrets on to them'. They 'sit down on the table by the writer, following his thought and gazing at him from the depths of their gold-flecked eyes

'A spooky cat playing with a ball' from an illustrated bestiary in a Latin miscellany produced in France, c. 1450.

with intelligent affection and magical penetration'. But what particularly fascinates Gautier is the cat's mysterious, occult 'nocturnal side'. With its phosphorescent eyes and spark-producing fur, it 'haunts the darkness without fear, where it meets wandering ghosts, sorcerers, alchemists, necromancers, body snatchers, lovers, thieves, murderers . . ., and all the gloomy phantoms that come out and work only by night. It has an air of knowing the latest news from the Sabbath, and it likes to rub itself against Mephistopheles' lame leg.' The yells that accompany its amours 'give it a sufficiently satanic air to justify to a certain extent the repugnance of diurnal, practical spirits, for whom the mysteries of Erebus have no attraction'.[15] Gautier's relish for cats' eerie, depraved tastes is of course largely affected; Madame Théophile and his other cats were in fact delightful domestic pets. Still, it did seem appropriate to project such feelings onto cats. Baudelaire, who also loved cats as domestic companions, showed similar perversity in exaggerating depraved tastes that he claimed to share with them.

We find the same attitude in the twentieth-century American writer H. P. Lovecraft, who loved cats and used them to express his ambivalence toward the horrors he wrote about. Appalling and perilous as these horrors are, sensitive, thinking people must be drawn to them because they are the reality underlying the bland wholesome surface that ordinary people see. Cats embody this attraction, while never pursuing horror to the point of becoming horrible themselves; they are eerie, but never repulsively so. They are at home in the world of nightmare, yet at the same time they are reassuring because they can be counted on as friends of man. Both the narrator of 'The Rats in the Walls' and his cat are fascinated by the mysterious horror that lies under the ancestral house, but the cat (unlike his corrupted owner) rejects it. In *The Dream-Quest of Unknown*

Kadath, the hero wanders among hideous horrors on the far side of the moon until, to his delight and relief, he hears the yowls of cats, who bring him back to earth. In his essay 'Something about Cats' (1926), Lovecraft made explicit the connection Gautier had implied between attraction to the demonic and admirable refusal to conform. Cats, he said, reject the conventional American's sentimental morality and foolish ideals of manliness and sociability, which dogs enthusiastically share. The cat lover proves his superiority by rejecting 'pointless sociability and friendliness, or slavering devotion and obedience'. Like the cat, he 'is a free soul . . . whose only law is his own heritage and aesthetic sense'.[16]

Several nineteenth-century writers of more or less realistic fiction contrived to exploit the cat's reputation for disturbing, mysterious powers without ranging beyond the bounds of possibility: they describe feline characters in such a way as to convincingly cause human observers to credit them with supernatural powers. The second black cat in Poe's story 'The Black Cat' (1843) seems to have preternatural knowledge and a conscious determination to punish the narrator for murdering its predecessor. Although the narrator was originally a kind man, he became so degraded by alcoholism that he took to abusing his once cherished pet, a black cat named Pluto. Pluto naturally began to avoid him, and, unwilling to face this evidence of what he had become, he gouged out one of the animal's eyes and finally hanged him. At first he was pleased when an almost identical cat appeared and made friends, but when it insisted on pursuing him with demonstrative feline affection, clambering and clinging even when he shrank from it, he came to feel that it was persecuting him with reminders of his former crime.

Although the second cat's behaviour could be entirely natural, it looks like a supernatural avenger. It seems to appear out of nowhere, and its resemblance to Pluto suggests that it might be his reincarnation. It drives the narrator to the crime that will destroy him: by weaving around his feet as he went downstairs, it provoked him to strike at it with an axe, his wife to hold his arm, and him to strike her down. He concealed her body behind the cellar wall and would have got away with the murder if the cat, who had been accidentally walled up with her, had not alerted the police by its howling. At the same time that it acts as a clear-sighted nemesis, the second black cat acts as an agent of Satan – punishing the narrator's abuse of the first cat by drawing him into further evil and then damnation: he exclaims that its 'craft had seduced me into murder'.[17] What the narrator experiences as sinister supernatural powers in the two cats are of course the morbid passions in his own mind; it is these, not the animals, that are diabolical.

Charles Dickens's Lady Jane in *Bleak House*, the large grey cat whom the sinister junk dealer Krook bought for her skin but saved because he found her so congenial, is deeply disquieting as she constantly follows and clings to him, slinks reluctantly from a dead man's room 'winding her lithe tail and licking her lips',[18] and stares avidly at Miss Flite's cage of birds. Together with Krook, she embodies the predacity that Dickens saw throughout his society. Their evil is accentuated by their resemblance to the witch and familiar of tradition. Krook's mysteriously obtained knowledge, air of generalized malignity and final exit by spontaneous combustion strongly suggest a witch; and Lady Jane is well qualified to be the animal who facilitates his contact with the powers of evil. Although Dickens personally liked cats, they are menacing in his novels. He intensified the cold evil of Carker, the villain of *Dombey and Son*, by constantly comparing him to a cat.[19]

In Émile Zola's *Thérèse Raquin*, a pet cat takes on sinister powers solely through a human murderer's projection. In this way, Zola could fit the concept of cat as supernatural accuser into a strictly naturalistic novel. Because Laurent, the murderer, was close enough to his peasant background to suspect that cats take a demonic interest in human sins, he came to see François, Madame Raquin's pet, as an accusing witness. Yet, at the same time that Zola dramatized the subjective reality of Laurent's guilty projection, he kept in view the objective reality that François was only an inoffensive, uncomprehending animal; that is, the small available victim that the cat has been through-out history.

Thérèse's husband, Camille, and her mother-in-law were too obtuse to notice even when she made love with Laurent in her husband's bedroom, but François saw: 'Dignified and motion-less, he stared with his round eyes at the two lovers, appearing to examine them carefully, never blinking, lost in a kind of devilish ecstasy.' Thérèse found this amusing, but Laurent, who disliked cats, 'felt chilled to the bone' and put the cat out. His discomfort is understandable, since a cat's calm eyes do seem to see everything without giving anything away or revealing a trace of sympathy. After the lovers drowned Camille, the cat's behaviour, while always realistic, exacerbated their guilt and anxiety. On the night of their marriage, they heard a scratching at the door and interpreted it as the efforts of the drowned man to enter, although it turned out to be only François. In a natural response to their terror and Laurent's hostility, François 'bound-ed onto a chair, where with bristling fur and legs stiff he stood looking at his new master with a hard, cruel stare'. Laurent interpreted this defensive attitude as threatening and attrib-uted it to an intention of revenge. Afraid to throw the cat out the window, as he would have liked, he merely opened the door; and the bristling cat – who was, after all, only a vulnerable little animal – 'fled with a squeaky miaow'.[20]

Although François becomes increasingly important in the human story as an embodiment of accusing conscience, he never ceases to be a naturalistic cat. We can still believe that Laurent sees him as a satanic nemesis, with his clear-eyed stare and eloquent body language, and a dangerous adversary: despite its size, a cat will not submit and will fight ferociously if it has to. François is the only character in *Thérèse Raquin* who is never belittled. Being a cat, he remains resolutely natural, untouched by the uniformly foolish society around him.

Spiritual and occultist movements in the later twentieth century have revived serious belief in witchcraft and supersensory powers, although these are no longer considered either demonic or agreeably shocking. As witchcraft has become an enlightened nature religion and extrasensory perception a benign expansion of the limits imposed by reason, cats may be prized for their supposed supernatural abilities. Marion Weinstein, a contemporary 'practising witch', gravely explains that the cat is particularly suitable for a familiar because it collaborates voluntarily, it can read your mind, and it likes ghosts. Fred Gettings declares in *The Secret Lore of the Cat* that cats have access to 'the etheric plane', 'a level of spirituality, normally hidden to human beings'; their faultless movements reveal 'the presence of an undiluted etheric force'. David Greene claims that they read human thoughts through telepathy (unlike the visual cues used by the pedestrian dog) and 'can hold highly intelligent and revealing conversations with their owners'.[21]

Like many magical creatures, a cat could bring good luck as well as bad, although possibly it did so with the devil's assistance. The *matagot* of French folklore, a black tomcat, made his owner wealthy. However, there are fewer benevolent cats than sinister ones in western tradition; and when cats help people, they always do so on their own terms. A French folktale, set in the days when cats were believed to be devils and a dozen were hung from the maypole each year, tells how a desperately poor young peasant resolved to catch a cat to sell for this purpose. But when he tried to seize a black tomcat, it sprang away and told him, 'Imbecile, go home instead of pursuing me, if you don't want to lose everything you own.' He did so and arrived just in time to put out the fire that was about to burn down his house. Afterwards he exclaimed, 'A cat that speaks is a sorcerer, but I can say I owe a handsome candle to that sorcerer.' 'You can say that again', said a voice behind him; there was the cat, licking its whiskers. 'Go away, cursed one', the peasant cried, making the sign of the cross, 'before I throw some holy water on you.' 'Holy or not, I don't like water', said the cat. 'You are ungrateful, but I'll still do you a favour. Listen well: you scratch the earth from morning till night and still haven't got lard to eat with your bread; and yet, there is a little corner here which could make you rich. You go there every day, but you despise it. Understand and look.' At first the man could not believe the cat, for he had turned and re-turned every inch of his land; but then he understood that it meant under the privy. Though he suspected the cat was mocking him, he was so desperate for money that he dug through the muck. Sure enough, he found a box full of gold pieces and jewels.[22]

In several other stories, cats with magical knowledge choose to form partnerships with human friends and expect their due reward. An old Irish woman who was spinning late into the night heard a small voice pleading outside, 'Ah, Judy, agrah, let me in, for I am cold and hungry.' Thinking it was a lost child, she opened the door, and 'in walked a large black cat with a white breast, and two white kittens after her'. They all went to the fire and warmed themselves, loudly purring all the while.

Then the mother cat warned Judy not to stay up so late, for the fairies had planned to use her room for a meeting and her presence prevented them; 'so they were very angry and determined to kill you, and only for myself and my two daughters here you would be dead by this time . . . So I ran on to tell you, and now give me a drink of milk, for I must be off.' After finishing the milk, she bid Judy, 'Good-night . . . You have been very civil to me, and I'll not forget it to you.' She took her kittens up the chimney, leaving a piece of silver on the hearth, worth more than Judy could make in a month by her spinning.[23]

'The Little White Cat', in a tale from Languedoc, makes the fortune of a woman who treats her right, but has no mercy on one who does not. When a lord with a haunted castle promises 1,000 francs to anyone who will spend the night there, an old woman volunteers and goes in with her little white cat and a leg of lamb. She cooks the lamb and shares it equally with her cat, who advises her how to keep the ghost from entering; and the woman gets the reward. But when her neighbour tries to do the same thing, she eats all the lamb herself and gives the cat only the bones. So the cat misadvises her and hides, while the ghost comes in and eats the woman up. The cat coolly saunters home and tells her mistress the story.[24]

The most famous of all feline magical helpers, 'The Master Cat: or Puss in Boots', retains the lowly status of a medieval peasant's cat despite his superfeline abilities. He is still the crafty trickster of *The History of Reynard the Fox*, although now he has merged with the clever servant of traditional comedy. A miller bequeaths his mill to his oldest son, his ass to the second and his cat to the youngest. The young man despairs – 'when I have eaten up my cat, and made me a muff of his skin, I must die with hunger'. But the cat assures him that, if he will only give him a bag and a pair of boots, he will make his fortune. The youth is not hopeful, even though he has observed the cat's cunning stratagems to catch mice; but he gives him what he wants. The boots might be a whimsical allusion to the bootlike markings common on cats' feet (like the 'socks' for which President Bill Clinton's cat was named), but more probably they suggest that Puss, like other fairy tale cats, was making a claim to human status.

The cat uses the bag to catch game and presents it to the king from his master, to whom he gives the fictitious title Marquis of Carabas. Ultimately he makes the king believe that his master is the owner of vast fields and a magnificent castle. The castle actually belongs to a rich ogre, whom the cat tricks into turning himself into a mouse, in which form he promptly kills and eats him. In the end the king offers the young peasant his beautiful daughter in marriage. Writing from the same underdog point of view as the author of *Reynard the Fox*, the author relishes the

Puss cajoles the ogre in Gustave Doré's illustration to *Puss in Boots* (1862).

unscrupulous cleverness of the cat, who effortlessly hoodwinks the king and the ogre and is, in fact, the only intelligent character in the story. True to the cat's independent nature, Puss does not tell his master what to do, as a dog or horse might, but acts on his own, confiding in no one. Puss's story was first written down in 1553 by the Italian Straparola and is best known in Charles Perrault's version of 1697.[25]

Arthur Rackham's illustration of Dick Whittington's cat demolishing the mice in a country where cats had been unknown (1918).

The cat legend was already attached to the historical Mayor of London in this portrait of Sir Richard Whittington (1350–1423) with a cat by R. Elstrack, c. 1618.

A cat's natural dexterity in catching mice takes on a supernatural aura when it is introduced into a country where cats were unknown and the people are desperate because they have no way to control the mice that are swarming over their food supply. The British version of this story has been artificially attached to the medieval Mayor of London Richard Whittington, but it exists in 26 countries.

Dr Seuss's *The Cat in the Hat* (1957) is a modern version of a magic cat. He brings excitement and anarchy into the lives of two children who are alone at home with nothing to do on a dull rainy afternoon. He appears from nowhere with a magic box containing Thing One and Thing Two, and they all proceed to take the house apart, although he puts everything back

The Japanese *maneki-neko*, a popular image in Oriental homes and shops, beckons to bring in prosperity.

together just in time with a magic straightening-up machine. His catlike disregard for authority and imperviousness to remonstrations make him a bit alarming, but he brings enchantment into the routine of everyday life.

In Japanese legends and folk tales, beneficent cats predominate over demon cats (foxes are more apt to appear as malevolent spirits). By far the most prominent good luck cat anywhere is the Japanese *maneki-neko* (calling cat), whose image appears all over Japan and has spread to Chinese and Chinese American businesses. It is a plump, friendly cat sitting up with one paw raised in the Japanese gesture of beckoning, and it brings customers into a store or general good fortune and prosperity into a household. According to the best account of the origins of this figure, supported by documents held at the Gotoku-ji temple in Tokyo, the temple was falling into ruin in 1615 and had practically no parishioners. One day the sole remaining monk, whose only companion was a cat he had rescued from starving, lamented, 'Kitty, I can't blame you for not helping, after all you're just a cat. If you were but a man, you might do something to help us.' Soon after, a lord with his retinue were caught in a violent storm near the temple. When he saw a cat sitting by the temple gate beckoning to him, he took shelter there. Impressed by the wisdom of the monk and touched by the state of the building, he made it his family temple. From then on, the temple prospered, and cats are honoured there. They are buried in the cemetery, and cat souvenirs are sold in the temple and neighbourhood.[26]

In a similar story, a cat came regularly to sit by the famous late medieval artist Cho Densu in the monastery Tofuko-ji, where he was painting an enormous picture of the entrance of Buddha into Nirvana. One day he ran short of ultramarine blue, and he joked to the cat, 'If you would be good enough to procure for me the mineral [lapis lazuli] powder that I need, I will portray you in this painting of Nirvana.' The next day, the cat not only brought him some powder but showed him where an ample supply could be found. In recompense, the artist included the cat in his composition, and thereby improved its moral reputation throughout the country. This rehabilitation was important, because in Buddhist tradition the cat was often disparaged as impious for showing disrespectful unconcern when Buddha ascended into Nirvana.[27]

The *maneki-neko* is most often a calico cat, predominantly white with black and red-brown spots. Sailors particularly favoured such cats, believing that they could foresee a coming storm and also, by climbing up the mast, drive away the ghosts of drowned people, which drifted constantly on the waves. Sailors tried to bring one along on every voyage.

In Thai tradition, the image of the cat is even more positive. The *Tamra Maeo Thai* (Treatise on Cats) lists seventeen types of auspicious cat, who, if treated right, will bring prosperity to their owners. This treatise carried more authority than simple folklore: its precepts were so highly esteemed that they were versified and written down by scholars and then preserved in palaces and temples. Although the extant manuscripts date from the nineteenth century, the lore they record is much older. The *Tamra Maeo*,

Kao Taem (Nine Spots), an auspicious cat from the *Tamra Maeo Thai*, a 19th-century manuscript of traditional cat lore. Notice the characteristic feline leg markings that, in European cats, inspired 'Puss in Boots'.

Wichian Mat (Moon Diamond), an auspicious cat from the *Tamra Maeo Thai*. Though one of many varieties of cat in Thailand, it was introduced in Europe as the Siamese cat. European breeders drastically modified its head shape and build.

which exists in several versions, describes and pictures the seventeen good cats – the solid black, twelve black and white combinations, the 'copper' (actually solid brown, like our Burmese), the solid grey (our Korat), the white, and the light-coloured with dark points (our Siamese). Breeding and nurturing these cats will bring a family health, wealth, slaves and retainers, power and high rank, and will keep away enemies. A black cat with white ears will bring success in studies. Of course these animals must be treated well. You must not despise your cat, 'or hit it, but take care of it with love / Give it fine food, rice and fish.' When it dies, you must bury it properly and continue to make food offerings to its

Thupphalaphat (Weakness, Handicap), an inauspicious cat from the *Tamra Maeo Thai*. Unabashed and jaunty, it carries off a stolen fish.

Pisat (Demon), an inauspicious cat from the *Tamra Maeo Thai*. She is devouring her own kitten.

spirit. Despite their magical gifts, these cats are depicted as friendly pets, looking up with the engagingly self-confident expressions of prosperous cats certain of good treatment.

It is true that readers were also urged not to love or care for cats that differed from the book's descriptions. There were several unlucky cats that caused their owners to lose wealth and rank. These included albinos and tabby cats, but were defined largely by their bad behaviour. They constantly stole fish; they ate their kittens or bore dead ones; they skulked in outbuildings, fled from people and had a malevolent character. The tabby cat had the wildness, as well as the stripes, of a tiger. Auspicious cats, on the other hand, tended to be 'good in actions and manners'.[28] Despite the warnings against bad cats, who would have been a minority – albinos are a rare mutation, and tabbies are less common in Asia than in the West – these treatises must have reinforced a positive attitude toward cats and encouraged people to treat them considerately.

Even the most sympathetic European cat stories do not credit the animals with loyalty and devotion. But there are several such tales in Asia. Usugomo, a beautiful courtesan in seventeenth-century Japan, doted on her cat, Tama, and carried him along on her evening walks. Their close intimacy came to provoke nasty rumours, and Usugomo's master flew into a rage and chopped off the cat's head. Nevertheless, the cat retained such devotion and gratitude to his mistress that his disembodied head latched onto the throat of a snake that was menacing her and killed it. Cats who risk their lives to kill ferocious rats as big as themselves constantly appear in legends and pictures. One temple has the tomb of a cat that gave its life to defend the sacred precincts against a huge rat that lived there under the form of a beggar.

The beloved black cat of a desperately poor old couple turned herself into a geisha, taking the name of Okesa, in order to recompense them for their sacrifices for her over the years. She was successful and made much money for them, but at considerable cost; for, although she did not mind entertaining her customers and was a superb dancer, she disliked having sex with them. One day one of her customers caught sight of her in her cat form, eating; but she made him promise not to reveal her secret. When he could not resist doing so, an enormous black cat appeared from a cloud and snatched him from view.

In another tale, a fishmonger who did business with a money-changer in Edo regularly gave a bit of fish to the man's cat. When he got sick and was unable to make his rounds, he was puzzled but very relieved to wake up one morning to find two gold coins by his futon. After he recovered, he went back to the money-changer's and was surprised not to find the cat waiting for his treat. He learned that the money-changer had caught the cat taking coins and killed it. The fishmonger told the man that the cat had taken the money to repay his kindness; the money-changer was remorseful and erected a monument to the generous cat. A similarly misjudged cat is celebrated in a famous Thai story. A woman came home and could not find her baby anywhere; all she saw was her cat, with blood around its mouth. She leapt to the conclusion that the cat had killed her child and got her husband to kill it forthwith. Only then did she discover the baby safe, with the dead body of a snake nearby, and realize too late that her cat had saved her baby by killing the snake that threatened it.[29] In India, where cats are not generally kept as pets, the animal hero is a mongoose. In medieval Europe, where dogs were often idealized and cats never, the misjudged animal hero is the hound Gelert.

3 Cherished Inmates of Home and Salon

For many centuries after the decline of ancient Egypt, almost no one thought of the cat as a pet or companion. Apparently the first person to express attachment to a cat in writing was a ninth-century Irish monk, perhaps because his vow of poverty precluded his having any other animal to make friends with. He enlivened his scholarly labours by watching his cat, Pangur Ban (Beautiful White Pangur), and composed a poem celebrating their kinship. Pangur pursues mice as the scholar does truth: because they both love their work, they do not care about fame and are never bored; Pangur rejoices in his dexterity when he catches a mouse, just as the scholar does when he elucidates a difficult text. The two comrades work harmoniously, in silence because both are competent at their trade. The monk perfectly catches the combination of self-sufficiency and comradeship possible between human and cat, and he recognizes the kinship between God's creatures that orthodox church doctrine of his time denied.

The French poet Joachim du Bellay so loved his cat Belaud that he wrote a 200-line epitaph for him (*c.* 1558). Knowing that most of his contemporaries would think it ridiculous to mourn a cat, he made his poem slightly parodic by deliberately overstating his grief and enumerating his cat's beauties in the manner of a conventional poet celebrating his mistress. Nevertheless, his long list of lovingly recalled details must have been produced by warm affection. He cannot express what Belaud, a tiny 'masterpiece of nature', meant to him; he celebrates the cat's silver gray coat and the 'white expanse of ermine' he would display when he lay on his back, 'the sprightly grace' with which he would pounce on a rat, and the way he would 'Scamper, and skate, and prance / After a ball of thread', and then, when he had dragged it into a ring shape, would sit solemnly in the middle, 'Showing his fluffy round / Of paunch'. Michel de Montaigne, who loved animals and questioned smug assumptions about human superiority, chose his cat as evidence that the other animals do not exist merely for human convenience: 'When I am playing with my Cat, who knows whether she have more sport in dallying with me, than I have in gaming with her? We entertaine one another with mutually apish trickes. If I have my houre to begin or to refuse, so hath she hers.'[1]

But these men were rare exceptions. The idea that cats could be elegant creatures entitled to the same privileged treatment as high-bred dogs was novel when it began to spread in aristocratic circles in late seventeenth-century France. Two fairy tales given literary form at this time neatly bring out the changing attitude toward cats. Perrault's 'Puss in Boots' (1697) has remarkable abilities, but he is a sly trickster who serves a peasant. Mme d'Aulnoy's 'White Cat' (1698) not only has magical powers, but is so charming and polished that a handsome prince falls in love with her. She is an exquisite little aristocrat who fascinates the hero with the witty conversation of a salon hostess, and he shows his discrimination and good breeding by treating her with the ceremonious gallantry she deserves. After a year with her, he actually 'regretted sometimes that he was not a cat, so that he could pass his life in this good company'. He loves her so dearly that, rather than leave her, he asks her either

G. P. Jacomb-
Hood, illustration
to 'The White Cat'
(1889).

to 'become a woman, or make me a cat'.[2] When the cruel spell
is at last broken and the cat reverts to her true identity as a
princess, the change is in appearance rather than essential
nature. (In the folk tale original of 'The White Cat', the cat acts
like a clever animal helper rather than a lady, and the young
man she helps is the despised underdog of three brothers,
rather than the most handsome, brave and sophisticated.)

It became fashionable to pamper cats. A celebrated harpist,
Mademoiselle Dupuy, credited a cat with keeping her up to the
mark as a musician by indicating any mistakes as it listened attentively to her practice sessions; and she left her estate to her two
cats with meticulous directions as to how their meals were to be
served. Antoinette Deshoulières, an acclaimed poet at the court of
Louis xiv, wrote epistles to her friends and their cats under the
name of her cat, Grisette. The eighteenth-century English aesthete
Horace Walpole shared his French friends' affection and esteem

for cats (as well as toy dogs). He describes a supper given by a charming French lady, where 'there was but one of us that had four feet; he was in the shape of an Angola cat, but as gentle, sensible and agreeable as his mistress . . . He is the Duc de Nivernois's particular friend.' He reports to Mary Berry, whose cat he is keeping: 'Pussy and I have no adventures: now and then a little squabble about biting and scratching, but no more entertaining in a letter, than the bickerings between any husband and wife.'[3]

Jean-Baptiste Perronneau, *Woman with Cat*, 1747, oil on canvas: two haughty aristocrats.

During the eighteenth century, cats became accepted as pets among the middle class as well as an aristocratic coterie. Richard Steele's fictitious narrator in *The Tatler* (1709) enjoys coming home to the enthusiastic greetings of his 'little Dog and Cat', who bid him, 'welcome, each of 'em in his proper Language'. The French poet Jacques Delille insisted that his Raton proved that cats were capable of love and described him charmingly soliciting a bit of his master's dinner, or, with arched back and waving tail, offering his soft fur to be petted, or playfully pushing aside the hand and pen that compose these verses in his honour. The antiquary William Stukeley memorialized his cat in 1745, celebrating her 'inimitable ways of testifying her love to her master and mistress', recalling the pleasure of her companionship as he smoked his contemplative pipe, noting that she gave him 'much pleasure, without trouble' and that he could not bear to look at the place in his garden where she was buried. Christopher Smart had particular reason to appreciate his cat, Geoffry, who kept him company when he was confined in a madhouse. In *Jubilate Agno* (*c.* 1760), he elaborately demonstrated that Geoffry was a creature of God rather than the devil, praised his dexterity ('he is the cleanest in the use of his fore-paws of any quadrupede'), and lovingly listed the tricks he would perform.[4]

Samuel Johnson kept and loved a series of cats. He would personally go out to buy food for Hodge, James Boswell reports, lest his servant should feel imposed upon and consequently take a dislike to the cat. Boswell describes Hodge

scrambling up Dr Johnson's breast, apparently with much satisfaction, while my friend smiling and half-whistling, rubbed down his back, and pulled him by the tail; and when I observed he was a fine cat, saying, 'Why yes, Sir, but I have had cats whom I liked better than this;' and then as if perceiving Hodge to be out of countenance, adding 'but he is a very fine cat, a very fine cat indeed'.[5]

This touching consideration for Hodge's feelings shows not only Johnson's kindness, but his perception that a cat has quasi-human sensibilities that ought to be respected.

Boswell admits that he suffered from Johnson's intimacy with Hodge, since he was an ailurophobe who felt uneasy if a cat was in the room. Years before, Jean-Jacques Rousseau, another cat lover, had shrewdly attributed Boswell's dislike to his 'despotic instinct'. Domineering men 'do not like cats because the cat is free and will never consent to become a slave. He will do nothing to your order, as the other animals do.'[6]

Unfortunately for the image of cats, their acceptance as pets brought them into direct competition with dogs and thereby infuriated some dog lovers. Georges Louis Leclerc Buffon sneered at those who 'foolishly keep cats for their amusement' and turned the articles on the dog and the cat in his great *Natural History* into a panegyric on the first and a diatribe against the other. The dog 'possesses every internal excellence which can attract the regard of man'; namely, he thinks only of pleasing his master, waits eagerly for orders, calmly suffers bad treatment and promptly forgets it, and even strives to conform to his master's tastes and habits. If this is the standard for animal excellence, the cat's deficiencies are obvious. It is 'an unfaithful domestic', kept only because rats and mice are even more unpleasant. Even kittens, though superficially attractive, reveal 'an innate malice, and perverse disposition, which increase as they grow up, and which education learns them to conceal, but not to subdue. From determined robbers, the best education can only convert them into flattering thieves', expert at concealing their designs, seizing opportunities, and escaping punishment. 'They have only the appearance of attachment or friendship' and betray their disingenuity of character 'by the obliquity of their movements, and the duplicity of their eyes. They never look their best benefactor in the face; but, either from distrust or falseness, they approach him by windings, in order to pursue caresses.' Their feelings are self-interested, and their affection conditional. Cats do not 'properly pursue' their prey, but sneakily 'lie in wait, and attack animals by surprise; and after sporting with them, and tormenting them for

'Le Chat domestique', from Georges-Louis Leclerc, Comte de Buffon's *Histoire naturelle* (1749–67).

a long time, they at last kill them without any necessity, and even when well fed, purely to gratify their sanguinary appetite'. 'Even the tamest cats are not under the smallest subjection . . . for they act to please themselves only.' Buffon is outraged by the cat's refusal to behave like a properly conducted domestic animal: that is, to subordinate itself to its master's wishes, to abjure any inner life of its own and to relinquish to humans such privileges as hunting for pleasure. His bias even leads the distinguished zoologist to deviate from observable fact, notably when he castigates an animal noted for its exceptionally direct gaze for refusing to look people in the face.[7]

Buffon's attitude would have been conventional in the sixteenth century; in the nineteenth, it would have been extravagantly idiosyncratic. Cats had come to be generally accepted as charming and lovable over the intervening three centuries, and they were often grouped with dogs as our closest animal companions. Matthew Arnold's 'Poor Matthias', an elegy on his daughter's canary, is a sympathetic meditation on our relationships with all our companion animals, but distinguishes between birds and dogs and cats, whose powers are 'Nearer human' and whose lives are 'Closer knit . . . with ours.' In a letter to his mother, he described his cat Atossa 'stretched out on the floor by me, letting the sunshine bathe all her deep, rich, tawny fur over her stomach; her ways are beautiful'. Charles Dudley Warner wrote a fine appreciation of a cat's reticent

Edward Lear, in a letter of 1876, describes a vacation he was enjoying with his cat, Foss.

Mark Twain with a kitten friend, 1907. Twain loved cats and found them morally more attractive than humans.

friendship in his obituary 'Calvin, A Study of Character' (1880). 'When we returned from an absence of nearly two years', Warner recalls, 'Calvin welcomed us with evident pleasure, but showed his satisfaction rather by tranquil happiness than by fuming about [as a dog would]. He had the faculty of making us glad to get home.' Although Calvin liked companionship, he would quietly extricate himself from imposed familiarity: 'If there was any petting to be done . . . he chose to do it. Often he would sit looking at me, and then, moved by a delicate affection, come and pull at my coat and sleeve until he could touch my face with his nose, and then go away contented.' Calvin was a friend of Harriet Beecher Stowe's Juno and of the numerous cats in the Samuel Clemens household. Thomas Hardy's epitaph 'Last Words to a Dumb Friend' (1904) precisely articulates the emotional importance of a little cat to the family that mourns him. The death of this 'timid pensioner of us Powers' has left the author 'forsaken':

> And this home, which scarcely took
> Impress from his little look,
> By his faring to the Dim
> Grows all eloquent of him.[8]

Scrupulously avoiding overstatement, Hardy convinces us how deeply he cared about the quiet, unobtrusive creature that had graced his home.

It would be hard to find a major nineteenth-century French writer who was not particularly fond of cats. The historian Hippolyte Taine, the 'friend, master, and servant' of three cats, dedicated twelve sonnets to them in 1883. Stéphane Mallarmé doted on his Neige, who 'rubs out my verses with her tail, walk-

Caricature by Nadar of Théophile Gautier, 1858. Gautier was even fonder of cats than most French writers of his time.

ing on my table as I write'. Théophile Gautier's love of cats was notable even in his ailurophiliac time and place. One of his favourites, Madame Théophile, was 'so called because she lived with me on a footing of conjugal intimacy', following him everywhere and at mealtime often hooking morsels 'on their way from my plate to my mouth'. He recounts her hilarious first meeting with a parrot: at first she concluded the bird was a green chicken and proceeded to stalk it, but when it began speaking, it upset all her preconceptions and sent her panic-stricken under the bed. 'It is no easy matter to win a cat's love', Gautier declares; but 'if you prove worthy of their friendship', they will give you the same faithful companionship and intelligent affection that are conventionally expected from dogs.[9]

Illustration to E.T.A. Hoffman's *Murr the Cat and His Views on Life* (1819–21). Hoffman presented this autobiographical work as written by his beloved tomcat, Murr.

People who loved cats observed them so carefully and sympathetically that they could articulate what was going on in their minds, as Pierre Loti showed in his precise, sensitive description of two tomcats meeting on a rooftop. 'A white-and-yellow cat is lying close to the edge of a house-top', not asleep, but engaged in idle reverie. 'Suddenly, at the corner of a neighboring gable, a pair of erect ears are seen issuing from behind a chimney, then a pair of alert eyes, followed by an entire head: another cat!' The newcomer, a black cat,

> perceives the first cat from behind, and immediately stops short to reflect; then, in a series of counter-movements, very carefully planned, he steals nearer, advancing his velvety paws one after the other with ever-increasing caution. All the same, the yellow-coated day-dreamer is conscious of the other's approach, and suddenly turns his head: ears completely drooping, the faint outline of a grimace on his lips, an imperceptible preparing of claws beneath his soft furry skin.

However, 'Evidently these two cats are slightly acquainted, and have already a certain esteem for each other'; and therefore a duel does not ensue.

> The black continues to approach with the same skilful, sidelong movements, the same prolonged pauses; then, when he has come to within a couple of feet of his yellow friend, he sits down and looks upwards as though to say: 'You see, my intentions are perfectly honorable; I, too, wish to admire this fine landscape . . .' Thereupon the other turns away his eyes and fixes his gaze on the distant scene, as a sign that he understands and has lost all sense

of mistrust; seeing which, the new-comer stretches himself out in his turn . . .

A few more glances are again exchanged; their eyes half close as though in a friendly smile, and finally, now that the pact of mutual confidence has been definitely signed, the two thinkers, paying no further attention to each other, speedily become absorbed in a blissful state of dreamy contemplation.[10]

Loti takes for granted that cats can make a contract; two centuries before, educated opinion would have considered such an assumption ridiculous, if not impious, and argued that this supposed inability proved they had no feelings that humans needed to consider.

Victorian novels reflect the general attitude that cats were valued companions. Pets of any kind seldom appeared and never figured as individuals in earlier novels, but in the nineteenth century dogs and cats were included as part of a realistic picture of domestic life. The personalities of the fictional cats, however, are not so richly detailed as those of the real cats in memoirs; and they function as adjuncts to bring out the characters of humans, whether by accentuating them or by eliciting revealing reactions. Retired Corporal Jacob Bunting's Jacobina in Edward Bulwer-Lytton's *Eugene Aram* (1832) comically reinforces the characterization of her human friend: both are equally self-centred, unscrupulous, comfort loving and skilful in manipulating others. Their attachment is real, but reflects their low social and moral status. Chattie, the splendid Persian cat in Mary Augusta Ward's *Robert Elsmere* (1888), belongs to the upper-class Leyburn sisters, but she represents lazy sensuousness in a novel that preaches strenuous moral effort. This amiable, comfort-loving animal brings out the character and the limitations of

John Tenniel, illustration to *Alice in Wonderland* (1865). Alice is trying to get information from the Cheshire Cat, who displays typical feline aloofness.

humans who lack ambition to improve themselves, and she is constantly seen with the least estimable member of the family.

Anne and Charlotte Brontë, who loved all animals and particularly sympathized with downtrodden characters, introduced cats into their novels to mark the difference between sensitive people, who consider the feelings of an animal regardless of its conventional status, and obtuse ones, who despise cats as the associates of women and peasants. The heroine of Anne's *Agnes Grey* (1847) is distressed by the plight of the village cats, who are in perpetual danger of being killed by the squire's gamekeeper for poaching or worried by the dogs of the squire's sons, who think it is fun to set their dogs on poor people's cats. The worthy curate Mr Weston rescues old Nancy Brown's cat from the gamekeeper and boldly tells the squire that this cat is worth more to Nancy than the squire's entire warren of rabbits is to him, and Weston welcomes the cat onto his lap, while his worldly rector, who cares no more for its feelings than for those of his poor human parishioners, kicks it across the floor. Robert Moore, the hero of Charlotte Brontë's *Shirley* (1849), shows his worth by considering the feelings of cats as well as dogs. While the cloddish curate Malone demonstrates his virility by pinching the ears of the aged black cat, Moore leaves her alone except for quietly encouraging any advances she chooses to make.

Even eerie Lady Jane in *Bleak House* is a cherished pet. When Krook talks to his cat or carries her around on his shoulder, we see a normal relationship between an old man and his only friend, which connects him with ordinary humanity. Feline suffering, regarded with callousness or even amusement in earlier centuries, is taken seriously. In Poe's 'Black Cat', the narrator's murder of his cat is entirely comparable to the murder of his wife. In *Thérèse Raquin*, when Laurent's hatred of the seemingly accusatory cat finally overcomes his fear and he throws him out of the window, the effect is heartbreaking. François's paralysed owner, Madame Raquin, sees what is going to happen but can do nothing to prevent it; and the cat, his back broken by his fall, drags himself along all night long, crying and moaning. The murder of François evokes more emotion than the murder of Thérèse's husband, Camille; and we respond to it as we would to a crime against a human.

Once cats became pets, their fond owners emphasized softness and affection over slyness and predacity. Unfortunately, the impulse to rehabilitate cats from the disparagement and imputations of past times can lead to an equally false sentimentalization. The mawkishly edifying nursery rhyme 'I Love Little

Pussy' dates from about 1830: 'I'll pat pretty pussy, and then she will purr; / And thus show her thanks for my kindness to her.' Late in the nineteenth century, some anonymous animal lover felt called upon to supply the lessons in kindness to animals that are missing from the actual New Testament by fabricating a purportedly lost gospel, *The Gospel of the Holy Twelve*. She or he paid particular attention to cats, who have so often been victims and who are not even mentioned in the Bible. Jesus rescues a cat from some idlers who are tormenting it, and he finds a home for a hungry stray. The author elaborates in an editorial note that Jesus evidently preferred cats to dogs because dogs have been 'taught by man to hunt and worry' and because cats have been 'maligned and neglected although the most loving, gentle, and graceful of all animals'. [11]

Frederick Richardson, illustration to 'Pussy-Cat sits by the fire' in *Mother Goose* (1915).

Pussy-Cat sits by the fire:
  How can she be fair?
In walks the little dog:
  Says: "Pussy, are you there?
How do you do. Mistress Pussy?
  Mistress Pussy, how d'ye do?"
"I thank you kindly, little dog,
  I fare as well as you!"

A homely 19th-century American cat is placed at the border between human civilization and the forest in R. P. Thrall's *Minnie from the Outskirts of the Village*, 1876, oil on canvas.

Growing affection for cats and the tendency to sentimental-ize away their aloofness and potential for fierceness led to iden-tifying them with the Victorian ideal of Home. The cat was still economically important as a rodent catcher, because modern pesticides and building standards had not yet been developed, but most writers preferred to present it as a hearthside spirit rather than as a killer of household pests. It became an embod-iment of domestic virtue – a high calling at a time when the

Advertisement for Guillot Frères milk, lithograph by Théophile-Alexandre Steinlen, 1895.

Jennie Yeamans, *Our Jennie*, 1887, lithographic poster.

pure and harmonious home was idealized as never before. Popular artists constantly included cats in their wholesome domestic scenes to reinforce family values. *The Happy Home*, a religious tract, is illustrated with a picture of a middle-class father reading a devotional book to his wife and four children. A cat stands in the foreground, obviously also listening attentively. She occupies the central position that she held in Renaissance religious pictures, but now she participates in the pious activity along with the rest of the family. A Chinese painting of the same period called *Joy in the Home* reflects the same attitude. In this idyllic domestic scene, a mother lies on a settee surrounded by five happy attentive children, while a calico cat sits on a stool in the right foreground appreciatively watching their harmonious interaction.

Ancient Egyptian sculptors, medieval stonecarvers and seventeenth-century painters had celebrated mother cats' devotion and careful education of their kittens, but now the emphasis shifts from their courage in defending their young and their conscientiousness in teaching them survival skills to qualities more appropriate to the Victorian mother. A print titled *Three Little White Kitties (Their First Mouse)* reduces to vacuous prettiness a family of cats engaged in the serious business of instruction in mouse catching. Their round eyes overwhelm small mouths and tiny teeth, so that not one, including the mother, could possibly be a predator. Families of playful kittens, generally supervised by a benevolent mother, became a stock subject for painters. The kittens are engaged in the mildest form of mischief: they never break or steal, as they did in seventeenth-century still lifes, rather, they tiptoe around a formally set table, investigating the place settings without disarranging anything. The cat's habitually quiet behaviour and deftness of movement,

A typically sentimentalized 19th-century image: *Kittens Playing with Thread*, chromolithograph, c. 1898.

Cartoon of cats
destroying a
kitchen by George
Cruikshank. The
image of the cat
as an orderly
domestic spirit
was not universal
even in 19th-
century England.

which contrast so strongly with the boisterousness of the dog,
were conventionally interpreted as instructive models of orderly conduct and care for property. Feline mothers became good
housewives, training their young not only to keep themselves
clean but to behave nicely in the house and take care of their
clothing. Eliza Lee Follen's mother cat in 'The Three Little Kittens'
(1843) deprives her kittens of pie when they mislay their mittens
and praises them for finding and washing them.

So identified did cats become with the gracious home that artists intent on attacking bourgeois domesticity have used cats to prove their point. A Russian painting of 1918, *The Russian Merchant's Wife's Tea*, depicts an overfed, self-satisfied bourgeoise with her equally overfed and self-satisfied cat. In *The Bluest Eye*, Toni Morrison savagely attacks cats as the favourites of black women who falsify themselves by internalizing white bourgeois standards. If these women who do not drink or swear or enjoy sex, who cultivate thrift and repress emotion, whose ambition is to behave properly and keep an impeccable house, can feel affection for anything, it is a cat. A cat 'will love her order, precision, and constancy . . . will be as clean and quiet as she is', and will offer her the tepid affection and mild sexual pleasure that she finds more comfortable than human love.[12]

When painters began to specialize in cats in the mid-nineteenth century (following dog and horse painters a few decades earlier), they emphasized prettiness, cuteness and innocuous liveliness, and often increased the sentimental appeal by anthropomorphizing their subjects. Louis Wain, the overwhelmingly popular cat artist of the end of the century, almost literally made cats into cute, innocuous little people. His images – spread over Britain in the form of postcards, nursery pictures and illustrations for children's books – both capitalized on and contributed to the popularity of cats. For 25 years, he busily drew cats engaged in every conceivable human activity, so long as it was middle class and respectable. Unfortunately, his cats were so popular because he purged them of the disquieting characteristics of real cats. All are softened into plump kittens with round heads and big round eyes, lively and mischievous, but apparently devoid of claws or fangs. Some postcards showing cats as quarrelling couples (*c.* 1908) make no attempt to show convincing anger, human or feline. If his cats are alert and concentrated,

The Naughty Puss: Louis Wain's anthropomorphic images, which present cats as cute, innocuous little people, were overwhelmingly popular.

it is not to catch prey, but to win a children's game. They delight in group activities.

Despite his sentimental falsification, Wain did love cats; and he believed that his interpretation marked improvement in their status: 'Our English cats', he said, were being bred away from 'the uncertain and unstable creatures of the tiles and chimney pots', with their lank bodies and long noses, and into flat-faced animals with artless expressions and temperaments 'of loving conceit'.[13]

Sentimental portrayals of cats continue to appeal to people today, on everything from calendars to T-shirts. Up to the 1980s, American greeting cards almost always portrayed cats as pretty and sweet or pretty and cute. The great majority are kittens, drawn even more big-eyed and fluffy than kittens actually are;

generally they gaze attentively at their mistress or the viewer, rather than showing any interest in the outside world. In George Selden's extremely popular *The Cricket in Times Square* (1960), Harry the Cat behaves like an unusually nice little boy; when he joins his friends Chester the Cricket and Tucker the Mouse for a picnic, he eats not them but tidbits gathered by the mouse. When a hungry young cat arrives at a hotel in Esther Averill's *The Hotel Cat* (1969) and gets a handout from Mr Fred the Furnace Man, he longs to make himself useful in return. He takes over the job of greeting cat guests and worries whether he is doing it well.

Writers for adults, also, may be carried away by their affection for cats to endow them with preternatural tenderness and sensitivity. Paul Gallico claims to know many charitable cats that will gladly share their meal with a hungry stranger off the street. Winifred Carrière remarks that, when her writing is not going well, her cats try to comfort her with extra paw-pats and ankle-rubs. The homeless cat that makes her bed in the straw of a crib in Sylvia Townsend Warner's 'The Best Bed', is, the story

In the Rogue's Gallery, c. 1898: a photographic equivalent to the cutesy anthropomorphism of Wain's drawings.

implies, inspired by piety rather than the attractive soft crunch-iness of the straw. In 1988, Susan DeVore Williams compiled a whole anthology of stories in which cats strengthen the Christian faith of humans. Paul Corey proves that cats follow human conversations by assuring his readers in *Do Cats Think? Notes of a Cat-Watcher* (1977) that his cat brought in a rabbit unharmed on Easter morning because it heard him telling his daughter about the Easter Bunny the previous afternoon.[14]

The Victorian impulse to neutralize cats' natural wildness was less prevalent in France, where prominent writers such as Gautier and Baudelaire celebrated them as creatures of the night that yowled on urban rooftops and defied the law. In Grandville's anthropomorphic animal drawings (1840s), cats reflect the worldview of bohemian intellectuals who flouted domestic pieties and conventions. His cats' bodies are drawn in

Courting cat: illustration by Grandville to Balzac's 'Heartaches of an English Cat' (1842).

realistic detail, although their poses and costumes are human; and their faces display convincingly feline versions of innocence, sanctimoniousness, pomposity or lively sexuality. In one of his illustrations to Honoré de Balzac's 'Heartaches of an English Cat', in which a young virgin cat is used to satirize British prig- gishness and hypocrisy, the artless heroine stands between an angel cat wearing the characteristic serene feline smile and a big- eyed devil cat bursting with fiendish glee. In another, dashing, raffish tomcats court the demure heroine on the rooftops. Even in France, however, people valued their cats as household pets; Madame Raquin, an entirely conventional bourgeoise, loved her François. And cat lovers began to validate the worth of their pets by making them more like dogs. In the mid-1860s, the bulletin of the Parisian society for the protection of animals began to feature stories of feline fidelity. One even credited a cat with attempting suicide when his master killed himself.[15]

In Japan, cats were more consistently regarded simply as agreeable pets, neither exotically diabolical nor sweetly harmless. Kuniyoshi's many anthropomorphic cat pictures represent worldly scenes plausibly translated into feline form. In his *Elegant Entertainment* (*c.* 1840), a tomcat dressed as a merchant is attended by three demure geisha cats. One serves rice, one dances with graceful seductiveness, and one imperiously directs the kitten servant girl; despite their apparent concentration on increasing the male's pleasure, their sly expressions and laid-back ears suggest that their only real concern is their own self-interest. Pictures by Kuniyoshi and other artists of the *ukiyo-e*

In this woodblock print by Utagawa Kuniyoshi, *c.* 1840, the complacent tomcat patron and charming, demure, sly cat geisha are authentically human and feline.

school are often mildly subversive, as they parody refined social life and classical literary themes or represent people such as geisha and Kabuki actors, who inhabited the pleasure quarter on the margin of respectable society. Because cats are notoriously indifferent to human ideas of law and propriety, they are appropriate vehicles for mockery of bourgeois convention.

As cats gained in status, it seemed natural to apply to them the standards that were developing for dogs in the nineteenth century: namely, to organize cat breeds and breeding, validated by cat shows, as an equivalent to the newly established kennel clubs and dog shows. (Organized cat breeding goes back much earlier in Thailand, where the *Tamra Maeo* urged selective breeding to cultivate auspicious cats and eliminate inauspicious ones.) European and American owners did not disparage any variety of cat, but they did feel a need to regularize a population that varied in colour and shape, bred as they liked, and produced kittens whose appearance could not be predicted. People wanted to have pets with distinguished pedigrees (in some cases compensating for a lack in their own) and prided themselves on the antiquity of their cat's breed. Presumably the British Shorthair does trace 'its ancestry back to the domestic cat of Rome', since cats were brought to Britain by the Romans, but that hardly makes it an aristocrat.

Harrison Weir organized the first cat show at the Crystal Palace in London in 1871, and in 1895 the first official cat show in America was held in Madison Square Garden, New York. Systematized cat showing created a demand for pedigree cats, who could be depended on to produce kittens that looked like themselves; this in turn necessitated a system of registration, because a pedigree cat is defined as one with registered parents, grandparents and great-grandparents. Many cat clubs were

Edna B. Doughty and Louise Grogan with their Persians at a cat show in Washington, DC, in the 1920s. Persians have since been bred for flatter faces.

formed in Britain, each maintaining its own registration system; in 1910 they agreed to unite under the Governing Council of the Cat Fancy, which would keep the registers, license cat shows, monitor the welfare of pedigree cats and ensure that the rules were observed. The American Cat Fanciers' Association was founded in 1906, licensed its first two shows in the same year, and in 1909 published its first Stud Book and Register. There are now Cat Fanciers' Associations in many countries, and about 400 organized shows with rigorously trained judges are now held worldwide each year.

The organizers of the cat fancy were not activated solely by snobbery: this was their way to improve the status, and consequently the treatment, of cats. Weir expressed his hope in *Our Cats and All about Them* that the increasingly popular shows would bring 'the too-often despised cat' the 'attention and kind treatment' it deserved. Gordon Stables, another early promoter of the cat fancy, argued that good treatment would turn a meagre, furtive beast into 'a large, honest, plump pussy, with glossy fur and loving eye, that runs to meet you with a song, and jumps on your shoulder to have the pleasure of *giving* you the first caress', and expressed his hope that this sort of cat would soon be seen all over Britain. The United Kingdom's Governing Council of the Cat Fancy declares its 'strong interest in the welfare of cats, both pedigree and non-pedigree' and supports research on feline illness.

Nevertheless, one does question the purpose of defining 'exactly what colours and shapes' cats are to be, formalizing these as breed standards and rigorously training judges to assess individual cats according to the artificial standards. Moreover, as breed definitions become more precise, distinctions between breeds are inevitably overemphasized. As the Governing Council proudly notes, there was little difference in head and body shape between Persian and Siamese cats a hundred years ago, but now they are total opposites.

When Weir organized his show, he had to devise a system of breed distinctions, which were necessarily arbitrary apart from a few exotic breeds. Angora cats had been brought to Europe from Turkey in the sixteenth century and, in the nineteenth, Persian and Siamese cats arrived in Europe, followed by the Russian Blue and the Abyssinian. Siamese cats were included in the first show, but these modern darlings did not immediately charm the public: one journalist described them as 'an unnatural, nightmare kind of cat'. But native British cats had never been subjected to systematic breeding, as dogs have been, because they were already superbly adapted by nature to the task of rodent-catching that humans wanted them to perform. Breed distinctions among them could be based only on hair colour.

In an attempt to give depth to this classification, Stables attached personality characteristics to colour in his *Handbook* on cats. Although there might be some genetic linkage between colour and personality, Stables's breed descriptions are far more detailed and certain than the facts warrant. Moreover, they reflect Victorian preoccupation with moral worth and class, as well as the same determination to attach fine qualities to every breed that we see in the handbook of the American Kennel Club. 'The Black-and-white Tom cat', for example, 'is a large, handsome gentlemanlike fellow, a sort of cat that you could not believe would condescend to do a dirty action, or would hardly deign to capture a miserable mouse; and his wife is a perfect lady.' Brown tabbies, on the other hand, are creditable members of the working class: they 'are the true English cats, and, if well trained, possess all pussy's noblest attributes to perfection. They are docile, honest, and faithful, fond of children, careful mothers and brave fathers, though seldom taking advantage of their great strength.' Fortunately for cats, there was less emphasis on details of their appearance than we find in corresponding standards for dogs, although Stables did stipulate that for success in the show ring, the tabby's ears, especially the male's, must be short, and its stripes distributed just so. The American cat fancy groups all these colours as Domestic Shorthairs.

Alarmed when foreign breeds arrived in America and began to interbreed with the native cats, fashionable cat owners began a systematic breeding programme to fix and perfect the conformation and colouring of the original population. Like the British fanciers, they broke down feline beauty into a point system, with arbitrary specifications of proportion and pattern, but fortunately did not significantly alter the cats' appearance. In fact, the Cat Fanciers' Association concedes that the distinction between a pedigree Domestic Shorthair and a good-looking random-bred cat lies only in the fact that the former will more reliably produce kittens that look like itself. The Domestic

Shorthair was recently renamed American Shorthair 'to better represent its "All American" character'.[16] The British Shorthair looks much like it, but is supposed to be heavier.

Other breeds of cat, however, sometimes suffer from the same sort of single-minded breeding that has degraded many dogs. The natural cat's soft fur, perfect and functional shape, and sturdy health may be sacrificed to increase its value as a novelty or a status symbol. Breeds may be excessively elongated, like the Siamese, or excessively rounded and flattened, like the Persian. The original cats imported from Siam were light-coloured with the characteristic dark points, but had the normal feline head shape and muscular body. Westerners decided they should be thin and elegant, and bred for long noses and bodies slim to the point of fragility. Grand Champion Minghou's Dancing Slipper, the most recent Siamese best-in-breed in the United States, has an attenuated body, disproportionately long legs, tail and neck, and huge ears. The Persian winner, Grand Champion Artemis Stardust Memory, appears to be a mound of white hair, with a flattened face in which two big round eyes are the only marked features; it displays no evidence of feline alertness or agility. Persians do not like to jump or climb, and their flat faces make it difficult for them to eat, drink or even breathe normally.

Non-pedigree cats can be beautiful as well.

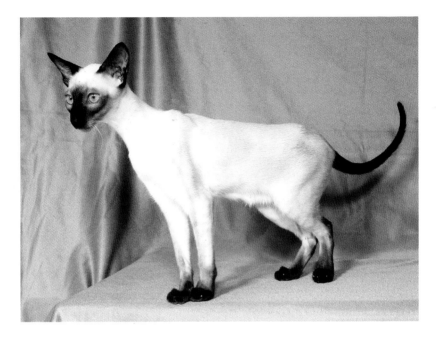

Supreme Grand Champion Saroko's Belles Starr, a prizewinning Siamese cat, illustrates the slim graceful elegance of the breed at its best.

Instead of being let to die out quietly, mutations such as crinkly hair, baldness and lop ears have been cultivated as novelties, so that we now have the crinkly-haired Rex, the naked Sphinx and the lop-eared Scottish Fold, with ears plastered tightly to its head. An uninformed cat lover would be apt to mistake the current champion Cornish Rex for an emaciated waif and take her in despite her ugliness because she looked so pathetic. The American Cat Fanciers' Association recognizes 37 breeds for showing in the championship class; the UK's Governing Council, who count different coat colours as separate breeds, recognizes 53.

These breed distinctions have taken on disproportionate importance, considering that the vast majority of cats one sees

Grand Champion Purrinlot's Seven of Nine, Distinguished Merit, displays her sumptuous coat and aristocratic bearing.

around are random-bred shorthairs. (The Governing Council proudly announces that it registers about 32,000 pedigree cats a year, but that is out of a total of 7,500,000.)[17] Yet a glance at the cat shelf in any bookstore shows that many cat enthusiasts find breed characteristics the most interesting aspect of cats. A large percentage of the books there are devoted to pictures, descriptions and (largely fictitious) histories of the various breeds.

4 Cats and Women

Cats have been associated with women from the beginning: Bastet was the goddess of maternity and female sexual allure. Despite a few exceptions such as Puss in Boots and Garfield, we still tend to think of cats as female and dogs as male; when we refer to these animals in the opposite sex, we must use the specialized terms *tomcat* and *bitch*. Spiteful old women are called *cats*; attractive young ones, *puss* or *kitten*. Small and soft, excelling in the beauty and grace that are supposed to be characteristically feminine, cats embody a charm that most women can only long for.

Once artists began to glorify worldly beauty in the Renaissance, they occasionally brought cats into portraits to highlight attractive qualities in human sitters. Often the resemblance is emphasized by similarities in colouring and pose. In Bacchiacca's *Portrait of a Young Woman Holding a Cat* (*c.* 1525), a brown tabby cat and a brown-haired woman in a black-and-gold striped dress gaze sidelong at the viewer with essentially the same expression: alert, rather wild and totally self-willed. The cat's flagrant animal vitality calls attention to the woman's implied sexual invitation. The sexual message is less direct in Jean-Baptiste Greuze's *The Wool Winder* (1759), where a pretty girl with a vacant, dreamy expression winds wool and an alert half-grown cat avidly watches her. The cat is poised for action and will soon snatch at the wool; it has also just reached the age

Jan Saenredam (1565–1607), *Allegory of Sight*, engraving.

when its vitality will burst out in sexual activity. By placing it beside the young human animal, Greuze suggests that there is latent physical energy under the girl's passive appearance, which will likewise find sexual expression.

Pierre-Auguste Renoir's paintings of luscious girls or women with equally luscious cats evoke a more generalized wholesome physicality. The cats are all lovely soft surface: there is no more

Francesco
Bacchiacca,
*Portrait of a Young
Woman Holding a
Cat*, c. 1525, oil
on canvas: two
attractive, wilful,
sexy animals.

Giovanni
Lanfranco, *Naked
Man Playing with a
Cat in Bed*, c. 1620,
oil on canvas:
a man plays the
courtesan's role,
abetted by a cat.

Pierre-Auguste
Renoir, *Young
Woman with
Cat*, c. 1882,
oil on canvas.

alertness, toughness or dynamic energy in them than in his
human females. In *Young Woman with Cat* (c. 1882), Renoir's
future wife dreamily watches a cat that delicately sniffs some
flowers. The two young subjects simultaneously exemplify and
enjoy the sensory pleasures of nature. They are equal in interest
and beauty; skin, hair, and fur are marvellously soft and appeal-
ing, and the tortoiseshell-and-white cat picks up the auburn of
the woman's hair and the white of her dress.

...a most provocative fragrance

MY SIN

LANVIN

More often, however, artists used cats to highlight the wiles and seductiveness of prostitutes, who have been called *cats* since 1400. As aggressively sexual animals that constantly groom themselves, female cats seemed the perfect emblem for whorish women. Cornelis de Man's *The Chess Players* (*c.* 1670) are clearly engaged more in flirtation than in chess. While the man seems passive, the woman turns around to look at the viewer with a knowing expression, suggesting that she is leading him on. A large tiger cat with an equally knowing expression sits on the

floor looking up at her, as if fully aware of what is going on. A cat with her rump suggestively raised stands in front of Moll Hackabout in Plate 3 of *The Harlot's Progress* (1732), and in N.-B. Lépicié's *Fanchon Awakes* (1773), a disreputable cat rubs against the shapely naked leg of the half-dressed young woman who sits on her messy bed pulling up her stocking. Women and cats are equally sexy and equally at home in the squalid scenes. The connection is even more obvious in Nathaniel Hone's portrait of the courtesan Kitty Fisher: beside seductive Kitty is a kitten hanging on the edge of a bowl trying to catch a goldfish; the predatory greed concealed under the woman's demure manner is explicit in the mischievous kitten. Édouard Manet introduced a lively black kitten into his portrait of the prostitute *Olympia* (1863) in order to emphasize her occupation, although its innocent, spontaneous sexuality contrasts with her jaded professionalism.

Alphonse Toussenel spelled out the connection between cats and prostitutes in his *Zoologie passionnelle* (1855): both animals are 'essentially antipathetic to marriage', are 'keen on maintain-

Raphael Kirchner,
*Extremities Touch
Each Other*, c. 1915:
feline titillation.

ing [their] appearance', are silky and shiny, eager for caresses,
ardent and responsive, graceful and supple, make night into day,
and shock 'decent people with the noise of [their] orgies'. He further revealed his hostility in his indignant assumption that both
of these undeserving animals enjoyed lives of constant pleasure
and leisure. 'Lazy and frivolous and spending entire days in contemplation and sleep, while pretending to be hunting mice . . .
incapable of the least effort when it comes to anything repug-

nant, but indefatigable when it is a matter of pleasure, of play, of sex, lover of the night. Of whom are we writing', he asks rhetorically, of the cat or of her human counterpart?[1]

In the early chapters of *Thérèse Raquin*, Zola directed sympathy toward Thérèse by describing her as a cat. Growing up in the stultifying Raquin household, she appeared passive, 'sitting silent and motionless on a chair with open but expressionless eyes. But when she raised an arm or put a foot forward it was possible to divine the feline litheness, the taut and powerful muscles, all the stored-up energy and passion lying dormant in her quiescent body.'[2] The image of a cat's outward stillness and violent potential graphically conveys the mental state of this intensely vital woman trapped in a circle of imperceptive, undersexed humans; the parallel suggests that she, like a cat, needs and should have freedom from such social constriction. But when he came to write *Nana* (1880), Zola threw away discernment and sympathy for his heroine or cats and fell back on the stereotyped cat-whore identification. The cats that fill the theatre where Nana works intensify its atmosphere of seedy sexuality. She herself is incapable of love and resembles a cat in her love of warmth and her manipulative caresses, as she rubs her chin against her lover's waistcoat to coax him into helping her get an unsuitable role.

Even when Zola's contemporaries really liked both cats and sexy women, the association still led them to suspect treachery and consequently to feel hostility as well as attraction. Men who celebrated the cat's mysterious nocturnal side, who praised it for alien depraved tastes and an affinity for evil, were also fascinated by unfaithful, destructive women. Identifying one's mistress with a cat, who does in fact have effective but usually concealed weapons and who does not requite human devotion with equal warmth, provided a convenient pretext for accusing the mistress of latent ferocity and coldness. Baudelaire's mistress Jeanne Duval was, at least according to his account, catlike in her gracefulness, her occasional cruelty and her passive acceptance of his devotion without understanding or responding to him. In 'The Cat' (the second poem of that name in *The Flowers of Evil*), his description of his intense sensual response to a cat mirrors his passion for her and his perception of her coldness. As he clasps a cat to his loving heart and luxuriously lets his fingers linger over her elastic back and electric body, he thinks of his woman. Her glance is deep and cold like the cat's, and cuts and rips like a spear. The dangerous aura of cat and woman enhances their charm.

Paul Verlaine's 'Woman and Cat' (1866) describes a woman playing prettily with her cat, soft hand and soft paw. But the cat has razor-sharp claws, which she has mischievously hidden (not simply retracted when they are not needed), and so has the woman, under her sweet manner. The cat's retractable claws, a simple evolutionary development to facilitate her method of hunting, have become a convenient emblem of her treachery – and, by an even greater stretch of logic, the analogy with a cat turns the charge of treachery onto the woman. These far-fetched comparisons have been repeated so often that, for some men, they appear to be self-evident truth. Thus E. V. Lucas casually writes that he feels proud when a cat singles him 'out for notice; for, of course, every cat is really the most beautiful woman in the room. That is part of their deadly fascination.'[3] Probably without intending to disparage, Lucas not only reduces beautiful women to nonhuman animals, but gives a superficial plausibility to the insinuation that female sexuality is dangerous to men: cats, after all, are dangerous – though only to the small animals that are their natural prey.

The hostility becomes unusually intense and overt in Guy de Maupassant's essay 'On Cats' (1886). As he tells of caressing a large white cat that interrupted his reading by jumping on his lap, he describes in loving detail her rolling, head-rubbing and kneading and his own delight in stroking her: 'Nothing is softer, nothing gives to the skin a sensation more delicate, more refined, more rare, than the warm, living coat of a cat.' But this is all a cover for fierceness and treachery, he goes on: 'She purred with satisfaction, yet was quite ready to scratch, for a cat loves to scratch as well as to be petted.' And this attributed hostility, in turn, arouses in him a 'strange and ferocious desire to strangle the animal I am caress-ing. I feel in her the desire she has to bite and scratch me.' The basis for this bizarre projection becomes clearer, if not rationally defensible, when he moves from the appeal of cats to that of attrac-tive women. Cats are 'delicious above all' because, while they rub and purr and look 'at us with their yellow eyes which seem never to see us, we realize the insecurity of their tenderness, the perfidi-ous selfishness of their pleasure'. In exactly the same way, when particularly charming, tender women gaze at us 'with clear yet false eyes' and 'open their arms and offer their lips' to a man, even as he 'folds them to his heart with bounding pulses' and 'tastes the joy of their delicate caress, he realizes well that he holds a perfidi-ous tricky cat, with claws and fangs, an enemy in love who will bite him when she is tired of kisses'.[4]

Whether this intense ambivalence came from individual psy-chological problems or the sadomasochistic strain in Romantic-ism that required love to be spiked with danger and hostility, it could be aptly expressed by identifying human female love-objects with cats. With their charm, their hidden claws, their sex-ual ardour and their cool self-centredness, cats provide a conven-ient metaphor for the alleged limitations of women's love; and human cruelty and duplicity can be projected onto cats. Sigmund Freud attributed men's fascination with serenely, unassailably narcissistic women to the fact that men have had to renounce narcissism as they grew up; women, he theorized, remain objects

of love because they retain their narcissism. People find cats charming for the same reason, even though lovers may complain bitterly of the coldness, infidelity and inscrutability of mistresses as well as cats.[5]

Our emphasis on the sexuality of cats, with the emotion we attach to it, is just one manifestation of our common human tendency to project our own animal appetites onto the so-called lower animals. Our attitude toward feline sexuality is unusual in its ambivalence, however. The lust we attribute to goats is simply disgusting. But though cats and cathouses may be squalid and immoral, catlike women are typically beautiful and desirable, even if they are prostitutes like Kitty Fisher. Even the slang words associating cats with human sexuality are not entirely distasteful. 'Pussy' is a vulgar word for something desirable. 'Tomcatting around' is more raffish than squalid. It is also remarkable that, despite the connotations of 'tomcat' and the obvious masculinity of the animal himself, men generally associate cats with female sexuality. Toussenel, for example, wrote as if all cats were female. Thus cats are used to help along men's historical tendency to project sexual desire they disavow in themselves onto women.

Balthus (Balthasar Klossowski), it is true, used cats to celebrate male sexual prowess; but the leering tomcats in his paintings are a notable exception to the conventional association of cats with femininity. He frequently painted girls and women spread out in vulnerable or provocative poses with a knowing tomcat gazing at a crucial spot. The woman in *Nude with a Cat* (1949) seems to be exposing herself to the almost humanly grinning cat lying on the bureau behind her. Balthus's gleeful cat-headed man in *The Cat at 'La Méditerranée'* (1949) is about to

Balthus, *The Cat at 'La Méditerranée'*, 1949, oil on canvas.

enjoy both the fish that are leaping onto his plate and the semi-nude woman who is approaching him in a canoe. The painter himself, however, seems to have longed for the tomcat's potency rather than identifying it with his own. In *The King of Cats* (1935) he portrayed himself as a fragile, jaded aesthete with a robust, happy tomcat rubbing against his knee. All of Balthus's tomcats suggest enviable vigour rather than degrading lust.

Although the Japanese do not take so moralistic an attitude toward geisha as Westerners do to courtesans, they do draw a connection between the abilities of cats and of geisha to bewitch men with their beauty, grace and artful (or sly) manners. *Ukiyo-e* artists paired cats with geisha, beautiful sexy women who are active at night and represent free pleasure rather than regular family duty and order. In a print by Kaigetsudo Dohan, *Courtesan Seated on a Box and Playing with a Kitten* (*c*. 1715), the kitten complements the subtly erotic pose of the woman, who extends a bit of her bare foot from under her kimono. Kuniyoshi's graphic depictions of sexual intercourse often include a cat sitting nearby and gazing with keen interest at the crucial spot. *Nekokaburi* (cat-like covering [of feelings]) means hypocrisy or feigned modesty and innocence; *nekonadegoe* (catlike speaking) means insinuation, persuading in a falsely sweet voice (analogous to English *pussyfooting*). Lafcadio Hearn, who lived in Japan from 1890 to 1904, was probably reflecting European attitudes when his observation that geisha always kept a *maneki neko* in their houses prompted his comment that geisha, like cats, are 'playful and pretty, soft and young, lithe and caressing, and cruel as a devouring fire . . . like the kitten, the *geisha* is . . . a creature of prey', though both may be delightful and lovable.[6] Native Japanese ambivalence toward seductive women is expressed most overtly in their folklore figure of the cat witch who conceals feline ferocity under the appearance of a beautiful woman.

Women, so often the objects of feline comparisons, rarely see cats in sexual terms. While there are almost always intimations of sexuality in male artists' pictures of women and cats, female artists lay less emphasis on pure physical appeal. In her austere portrait of *Sita and Sarita* (*c.* 1921), Cecilia Beaux used a cat traditionally insofar as it suggests feelings that the reserved woman controls; but these feelings seem to be eager youthful curiosity and demonstrative sociability. Pale Sarita, dressed in white, sits rather stiffly and gazes over the viewer's shoulder, while the inquisitive black kitten Sita, perched on her shoulder, engages the viewer's eyes with her golden stare. Yet Sarita's hand delicately steadying Sita on her shoulder suggests a real, though reticent, tenderness between them.

As men may use cats to censure women who seduce men but do not requite their love, women writers may use them to expose the selfish demands that men make on women. Cats, less sexually charged for women, can represent an independent life style that frees them from conventional gender roles and expectations. Sylvia Townsend Warner's Lolly Willowes is a middle-aged maiden aunt who is freed from her conventional life of service to others when a cat appears and leads her to become a witch. One day, feeling stifled by a monotonous life ruled by other people's claims, she appeals aloud for help and comes home to find a black kitten that claws her hand, licks his lips and falls asleep. She realizes that he must be a familiar and that she has made a compact with the devil, sealed with her blood. The animal, whom she calls Vinegar after a familiar described by the seventeenth-century witchfinder Matthew Hopkins, is plausible both as kitten and familiar. At first Lolly is wary of Vinegar, but his anxious mews and hopeful eyes soften her heart and she accepts him as a foundling. His destructive spells, aimed at forcing her nephew to leave the village, are

ineffectual because of his inexperience, this being 'probably his first attempt at serious persecution'.[7] Vinegar's role as a familiar is worked out with amusing verisimilitude, but even as a natural cat he inspires Lolly to begin living her life as she sees fit, independent of others' expectations and demands. She finds freedom in celibacy with a companion who will not restrict her. Contemporary practitioners of witchcraft as a serious religion see it as an expression of female self-assertion in opposition to traditional patriarchal religion.

Colette and Joyce Carol Oates use the male tendency to project human sexual feelings onto cats to bring out a man's selfishness toward his wife. The husbands in Colette's 'The Cat' and Oates's 'The White Cat' have morbidly intense feelings for the family cat because they identify her with a female human love object. Alain in Colette's 'The Cat' feels toward Saha, his Chartreuse cat, the way he should be feeling toward his new wife, Camille. Oblivious to Camille's feelings, he is acutely sensitive to every subtle sign of the cat's jealous misery over his marriage. Camille becomes uncontrollably jealous and, after a brilliant confrontation scene in which the female rivals manoeuvre against each other, impulsively pushes the cat off a ninth floor balcony. The cat survives, and Alain retreats with her to his family home. Alain assumes his preference for the cat is evidence of his refined tastes, and of course a cat can be more elegant, graceful and poised than any woman. On the other hand, a man should not have a cat's instinctive aversion to loudness and change, and he should not prefer cool feline liking to human love. Saha is the romantic ideal of a selfish man who prefers the simple relationship one can have with a cat to the demands of a mature relationship with a woman. In the end, we agree with Camille that, although her murderous impulse was evil and disproportionate, his devotion to the cat is abnormal; if she was a

Cecilia Beaux, *Sita and Sarita*, 1921, oil on canvas.

monster to have tried to kill an innocent, faithful little animal, he is a monster to abandon his wife for his cat.

While Camille is justifiably jealous of Saha, Oates's Julius Muir in 'The White Cat' is unjustifiably jealous of his wife's cat. Although he was far too civilized to admit this, he would have liked his attractive, much younger wife, Alissa, to care for nothing but himself. To prevent her from being distracted by children, he had presented her with a beautiful white Persian cat, Miranda, as a substitute. Nevertheless, he was gradually forced to recognize that Alissa would not give him the total devotion he demanded, a fact he first became aware of through the unconcealed indifference of her cat. Miranda was provokingly oblivious to his distinguished position in society. When he called her, she would regard him 'with indifferent, unblinking eyes'. In fact, she seemed to prefer everyone else. As he watched Miranda 'rubbing about the ankles of a director-friend of his wife's' and wantonly presenting 'herself to an admiring little circle of guests', he actually realized, to his own surprise and dismay, that he hated her enough to kill her. The cat seemed to be the embodiment of his wife's interests outside of him – perhaps the young director, perhaps just her newly revived career in the theatre and her friends there. Finally, his jealous fury mounted to the point that he came to identify the cat with Alissa herself and think that she deserved to die for not paying enough attention to him. After two failed attempts to kill the cat, he tried to kill Alissa, along with himself, by wrecking the car; but succeeded only in crippling himself. In the end he was blind and paralysed, listening to Alissa's sweet voice and living for those days when 'he would feel a certain furry, warm weight lowered into his lap'.[8] Has he been rightly punished for his jealousy, or do women allied with cats have eerie power?

Cats are also linked to women as homemakers, because women typically worked at home and cats typically stay around the house. And that is where they are supposed to be: as an old proverb had it, 'A good wife and a good cat are best at home.' For this reason, despite the convention that set cats in disharmony with sacred things, artists often introduced benign cats into domestic scenes with the Virgin Mary. In one of Barocci's portrayals of the *Holy Family*, a cat nurses her kittens on Mary's robe while she rocks Jesus. Clearly, the artist is suggesting a parallel between the two mothers. The sleeping cat in his *Annunciation* (1582–4) has a face as sweet as the Virgin's.

Having made the cat into a sweet hearthside spirit and an orderly homemaker, the Victorians set her up as a domestic model for women. Julia Maitland's *Cat and Dog; or Memoirs of*

Peter Huys
(c. 1519–77),
Annunciation,
engraving.

Puss and the Captain (1854) uses the animals to teach children their gender roles. Captain, a large sporting dog, learns to get along with a white kitten and to appreciate her qualities, so different from his own. They are both good animals; that is, eager to serve their master. But within that framework, they are the ideal Victorian man and wife. The dog, who tells the story, praises Puss for being 'gentle, graceful, and courteous . . . Always at hand, but never in the way; quick in observing, but slow in interfering; active and ready in her own work, but quiet and retiring when not required to come forward; affectionate in her temper, and regular in her habits – she was a thoroughly feminine domestic character.' (Her work, which of course is killing mice, is not specifically described.) She grows up to become 'the dear little companion who had formed my happiness at home', while he is established as her 'patron and protector'. Although Puss tactfully suggests that he restrain his aggressive impulses, she acknowledges that fighting is 'superior' to running away and spitting, and equates it with readiness 'to defend the weak, and to stand up for the right without fear of consequences'. 'There would be few great things done in the world if no one were more energetic or daring than I.' Puss resembles human fictional counterparts such as Dickens's Agnes Wickfield and Esther Summerson. The cat's natural unobtrusiveness, disinterest in human goals and small size are transformed into the human attributes of modesty, compliance, lack of ambition and timidity. There is nothing but praise for Puss, as for Agnes and Esther; but their virtues are manifestly inferior to those males can display. The effects of such thinking are evident in Philip Hamerton's ostensibly objective discussion of cats in his *Chapters on Animals*, where he credits cats and women with neatness, quietness and tact (physical in the case of cats, social in the case of women), and implies that these qualities by definition exclude the nobler ones found in dogs and men. Naturally, then, cats are the favourites of women and 'very intellectual', meaning effeminate, men.[9]

Images of Puss prevailed in greeting cards up until the 1980s. In traditional cards, cats almost always appeared with or represented females, who were typically shown in the home and happily performing domestic chores. Sometimes cats sit by the rocking chairs of nineteenth-century style mothers doing embroidery (a card of 1978); sometimes they perch on a pile of laundry that Mother may leave undone because it is Mother's Day (card of 1968). On another 1968 Mother's Day card, addressed To My Wife, a housewife cleans and cooks while a kitten watches, its head tied up in a bandanna like hers; inside, she sits in a skimpy cocktail dress, glamorously made up and holding a bouquet, while the kitten sits beside her smiling the same smile and wearing a ribbon around its neck. A cat wears an apron and a crown on a valentine for Mother (1975).

Cards for little girls served to prepare them for the same domestic role. Sweet, pretty, passive kittens accentuate and recommend the same qualities to little girls on valentines and birthday cards. In paired valentines for Daddy, the boy drives a locomotive with a cute dog riding behind him, while the girl sits in a chair contemplating a valentine with a pretty kitten looking up at her (1981). A perky white kitten gazes up at a girl graduate of 1969 to suggest that her scholarly achievement is less important than her feminine charm. Happily, cats, along with women, are beginning to escape from limiting stereotypes on contemporary cards: as women appear in nontraditional roles, cats are shown with men.

As good cats represent good wives, so bad cats represent bad ones. Medieval preachers constantly compared women who liked to walk out nicely dressed with roaming female cats.

Reporting on the scruffy cats of the London slums in *The Uncommercial Traveller* (1860), Charles Dickens found an opportunity to castigate the women who lived there, censuring the cats as sluttish housewives and reducing the women to feral cats. Like 'the women among whom they live', these cats

> seem to turn out of their unwholesome beds into the street, without any preparation. They leave their young families to stagger about the gutters, unassisted, while they frouzily quarrel and swear and scratch and spit, at street corners. In particular . . . when they are about to increase their families (an event of frequent recurrence) the resemblance is strongly expressed in a certain dusty dowdiness, down-at-heel self-neglect, and general giving up of things. I cannot honestly report that I have ever seen a feline matron of this class washing her face when in an interesting condition.[10]

Poster for David Belasco's comedy *Naughty Anthony*, c. 1900, lithograph.

Cover for *Harper's* magazine, 1896, reducing cats to elegant accessories of the good life.

The cats appropriately represent women because the most sacred obligations of both are attentive motherhood, orderly cleanliness and gentle behaviour. They provide an excuse for Dickens to express his obsession with negligent human mothers who reproduce irresponsibly and fail to take proper care of their children.

Don Marquis's Mehitabel, the battered street cat friend of his cockroach hero in *Archy and Mehitabel*, is also an unruly cat who stands in for unruly women; but he presents her with refreshing sympathy. Women were supposedly liberated from the domestic ideal by the 1920s, and yet their status and obligations remained much the same. Mehitabel is a typical feminist bohemian who wants to be liberated but finds that a female cannot escape being tied down by family obligations. A cat represents this situation perfectly, because at the same time that she is a free spirit disregardful of bourgeois conventions, she bears the sole responsibility for raising any kittens she may bear. 'Mehitabel tries companionate marriage' skewers the hypocrisy of radical males who preach sexual liberation for all but practise it only for themselves. 'A / maltese tom with a black heart and / silver bells on his neck' offered her 'honorable up to date / companionate marriage', and she couldn't resist, even though she knew that 'if its marriage / theres a catch in it somewheres . . . any kind of marriage / means just one dam kitten after another.' Sure enough, he left her flat as soon as the kittens arrived; and she has to conclude that companionate marriage is the same thing as 'old fashioned American / plan three meals a day marriage / with no thursdays off.'

Like any harried mother, feline or human, she tries hard but often unsuccessfully to be selflessly devoted. She cannot resist longing 'to live my own life' and protesting that 'it isnt fair / these damned tom cats have all / the fun and freedom.' Still, in the end she grimly resolves: 'self sacrifice always and forever / is my motto.' She 'will make a home' for her sweet innocent little kittens, and she determines to hope that no rain will fall and drown them in the abandoned garbage can where she left them before she can get back to rescue them.[11] The cool cat, oblivious

George Herriman, illustration to Don Marquis, *The Life and Times of Archy and Mehitabel* (1927).

to human ideology, can bring out the injustice of human standards that deny any conflict between self-fulfilment and motherhood, and assume that glad self-sacrifice is natural to women, although not to men. Through the relative artlessness of a cat, Marquis exposes the hypocrisy of women who refuse to admit any hostility to those for whom they must sacrifice themselves.

Artists portraying the Fall of Man, when Eve ruined mankind by acting independently instead of waiting for her husband's direction, often added a cat to emphasize her insubordination. Albrecht Dürer placed Eve and a cat together on one side of his

Fall of Man (1504) in order to suggest a parallel between the woman about to mislead her man and the cat about to seize the mouse in front of it. In his version of the theme (1616), Hendrik Goltzius portrayed Adam gazing besottedly at Eve, who looks seductively at him, while a large tabby and white cat with a knowing expression sits in the foreground.

As Dickens berated human slatterns by reporting on feline ones, Buffon berated insubordinate wives by abusing cats. The intensity of his moral attack on these animals can best be explained as displacement onto them of indignation provoked by women who refuse their husbands the obedience and devotion to which they consider themselves entitled. His description of canine and feline attitudes toward authority uncannily echoes discussions by his conventional patriarchal contemporaries of good and bad women. Neither domestic animals nor women were supposed to have interests or opinions of their own or to withdraw their affection if they were ill-treated.

Since men were supposed to derive authority over women from superior rationality, women who oppose men had to be activated by intractable perversity and wildness, qualities they share with cats. One of Aesop's most popular fables, 'The Cat Maiden', suggests this connection: a cat persuades Aphrodite to change her into human form in order to win a man's love, only to expose her incorrigible ferocity by leaping from her bridal bed to pounce on a mouse. Chaucer's Manciple uses the comparison to support his assertion that a woman will by nature betray the most considerate husband for a worse man, just as a cat will unhesitatingly leave the most comfortable home to chase a mouse. Both animals perversely prefer freedom to the most comfortable restraint.

Although modern men do not bluntly state that men should rule women because men are more rational, the medieval attitude persists. Ambrose Bierce facetiously defined Woman in his *Devil's Dictionary* (1906) as

> An animal usually living in the vicinity of Man, and having a rudimentary susceptibility to domestication . . . the most widely distributed of all beasts of prey, . . . the creature is of the cat kind. The woman is lithe and graceful in its movements, especially the American variety (*Felis pugnans*), is omnivorous and can be taught not to talk.

Like many jokes, this one covers a seriously held attitude, which is also seen in the supposedly scientific observations of early psychoanalysts. Sigmund Freud pronounced that women retard the progress of civilization, and Carl Jung drew the connection with cats: cats resemble women, he remarked, because cats are 'the least domesticated of the domesticated animals' in contrast to dogs and men.[12]

A cruder hostility to women is expressed in the deplorable 'I Hate Cats' books of the 1980s and 90s, although it is camouflaged as humour. Simon Bond's *101 Uses for a Dead Cat* (1981) includes a dead cat put to use as a pencil sharpener, standing on a desk with its tail up; a man sticks a pencil up its anus in a pretty obvious image of rape. 'Dr' Jeff Reid, author of *Cat-Dependent No More!*, repeatedly asserts that 'cat-dependency' is 'largely a female malady', which he attributes to the masochism that is natural to females. Dr Robert Daphne claims he was provoked to write *How to Kill Your Girlfriend's Cat* by resentment at having to share his girlfriend's attention with her cat. 'For thousands of years boyfriends have been killing their girlfriends' cats, clubbing or stoning them in Neanderthal days . . . using more devious methods as civilization arose . . . Remember, behind every successful relationship is a dead cat.' The cat must be killed because it is both a model of independence itself and an object of attachment that distracts the woman from total concentration on her man: once it is gone, 'nothing will stand in the way of you and years of happiness'.[13] Killing a woman's cat also brings to mind the possibility of killing the woman herself. Significantly, one of Daphne's exemplary cat-killing lovers is Henry VIII. This book would not have been so successful if its audience were restricted to passionate cat haters; it appealed to the larger group who fantasize about hurting women but prefer their misogyny to be lightly disguised. It spawned a sequel in 1990, *How to Kill Your Girlfriend's Cat Again*, which featured 40 more sadistic ways of doing the job, together with a promise of a third volume, *How to Kill Your Girlfriend*.

Cats conveniently represent what men have long and bitterly complained of in women: they do not obey and they do not love sufficiently. Men who cannot control women as they would like to, associate them with animals that cannot be controlled. Men who expect from women a devotion too absolute to be within human capacity, find coldness and concealed hostility in cats and attribute them to women as well. Identifying women with cats helped to fit both into easily defined roles and made it easier to accept stereotypes without thinking critically about the evidence. The association was used to censure wives for incorrigible insubordination or to reduce them to unobtrusive little homebodies. Cats enhanced the sexual allure of women, but also supplied images of passive softness or lasciviousness or cold unresponsiveness or treachery. The qualities that are simply natural in a cat are immoral in a woman, and their immorality in the human context redounds upon the cat's character. Men have typically used comparisons between the less esteemed sex and the less esteemed companion animal to discredit both of them.

While women tend to identify with cats, men tend to see and judge them from outside, just as they do women. They slide into generalizations that are necessarily reductive even when they are not overtly disparaging. Paul Gallico remarks that women manipulate like cats and are equally clever and artful in getting their way from a more powerful authority – forgetting in typical patriarchal fashion that such behaviour does not proceed from intrinsic nature, but from the fact that those in a weak position often have to manipulate in order to survive. Kinky Friedman speculates that 'women and cats have a lot in common' and proceeds to attach to women characteristics that cats share with all human beings: a preference for 'things that either comforted them or intrigued them', a liking for being 'stroked or cuddled', and a readiness to 'pounce when you least expected it'. When Gallico pronounces that 'No one ever really understands either women or cats', he isolates both groups from general humanity, represented by men. His allegation does not even make sense unless 'no one' is replaced by 'no man'. Liking cats too much to disparage them as inscrutable and treacherous, Konrad Lorenz manages anyway to force them into a comparison to disparage women: 'the cat is looked upon as false and "catty" because many similarly graceful women really deserve those epithets.'[14]

When one sex writes most of the books and paints most of the pictures, it is inevitable that the other sex is viewed as essentially different, and that the difference makes them inferior. The Chinese principles of yin and yang are both necessary for the functioning of the world, but yang, the masculine, heavenly, positive, bright, active principle, is clearly superior to yin, the feminine, earthly, negative, dark, passive one. In both China and Korea, men and dogs are yang, while women and cats are yin.[15] Just as in the West, women and cats may be good in their way, but it is a secondary sort of goodness.

5 Cats Appreciated as Individuals

Nowadays we are less apt to turn cats into symbols, because we are more apt to see them as individual members of the family. As we have become less comfortable with hierarchical order, we expect cats (as well as dogs) to be equal companions more than dependent inferiors. We are more ready to recognize rights, independence, even a sort of equality in the so-called lower animals. Seeing our cats and dogs as friends rather than property, we do not like to call ourselves their owners; and there is a vigorous movement in the United States to substitute the term *guardian*, both in common usage and in law. Cats reinforce this egalitarian tendency by appearing to assume an equality not claimed by other domestic animals. Cat lovers can now admire cats' independence and accept their self-interestedness and predatory impulses as we do our own. As traditional gender roles have broken down, we avoid simplistic identifications of cats with women. Because we now see cats as more like people, authors can portray relationships in which a cat is a person's best friend, can analyse the character of a cat they love, and can create convincing renditions of a cat's consciousness.

In contrast to Early Modern writers who reviled cats for their insubordination and Victorians who made them amiable by turning them into domestic spirits or cute children, there were a few perceptive nineteenth-century cat lovers who

Arnold Rothstein's photograph of the self-sufficent cat in snow, 1940.

extolled their self-sufficiency. François René de Chateaubriand delighted in the cat's

> independent and almost ungrateful nature, which prevents him from attaching himself to anyone . . . He arches his back when you caress him, but it is a sensual pleasure that he is experiencing, and not, like the dog, the silly satisfaction of loving and being faithful to a master who repays him with kicks. The cat lives alone, he has no need for society, he obeys only when he feels like it, he feigns sleep in order to see better, and he seizes everything he can seize.

Alexandre Dumas cheerfully accepted the cat as an unabashed 'traitor, deceiver, thief . . . egotist . . . ingrate'. Her egotism is proof of her superiority: the dog's willingness to hunt for man demonstrates his stupidity, while the cat has an excuse when she catches a bird, for she means to eat it herself. Mark Twain wrote that 'Of all God's creatures there is only one that cannot be made the slave of the lash. That is the cat. If man could be crossed with the cat it would improve man, but it would deteriorate the cat.'[1]

Rudyard Kipling's brilliant fable 'The Cat That Walked by Himself' in the *Just So Stories* is the classic tribute to the cat's quiet insistence on keeping true to himself. After Woman has

domesticated Man, Dog and Horse, Cat smells warm milk and presents himself at the cave. He persuades her to admit him by amusing her baby, putting it to sleep by purring, and killing a mouse in the cave – all of which he would have done anyway to please himself. Thus he wins his point without making any concessions: 'still I am the Cat who walks by himself'.[2]

Now it is common to celebrate cats for their amusing perversity, their refusal to comply with human wishes and standards, their emotional independence and their cool pursuit of self-interest. More and more people are appreciating cats for their unique qualities, rather than seeing them as inferior versions of dogs. Since about 1980, many of the cats on greeting cards have been comic and saucy rather than pretty and sweet. They are lithe adults rather than fluffy kittens, and their teeth are as prominent as their eyes. Instead of fitting in with humans or gazing adoringly at them, they tease them with smart aleck remarks. A cat on the front of a 2005 birthday card exclaims, 'Happy Birthday! I don't know what I did to deserve a sister like you.' Inside, it cries, 'But whatever it was . . . I'm sorry! I'm sorry!' A cat wearing a Santa hat on a 2005 Christmas card sings, 'O Christmas Tree, O Christmas Tree, Your ornaments are History!'

'A cat showing great interest in a mouse' from a Latin Bestiary made in England, c. 1170.

In 'An Assortment of Cats' (1893), Jerome K. Jerome cleverly analysed the methods cats use to win human favour by exploiting human vanity. The Chinchilla heroine explains that it is not difficult to secure the luxurious home that every cat deserves: 'Fix on your house, and mew piteously at the back door. When it is opened run in and rub yourself against the first leg you come across. Rub hard, and look up confidingly. Nothing gets round human beings, I have noticed, quicker than confidence. They don't get much of it.'[3] Yet, Jerome implies, humans are in no position to denounce cats, because we are not more altruistic than they, only more sentimental and self-deluded. If cats' interest in humans is to secure themselves a comfortable home, humans' interest in cats is to be flattered with the belief that they are kind, trustworthy and deserving of discriminating love. Feline affection can be even more gratifying than that of dogs, for, since it is less readily given and more likely to be withdrawn, we can interpret it as a validation of our particular distinction and sensitivity.

'Cats are, of course, no good,' Paul Gallico explained affectionately in 'My Boss, the Cat' (1952). 'They're chiselers and panhandlers, sharpers and shameless flatterers . . . full of schemes and plans, plots and counterplots, wiles and guiles.' Kitty 'wants attention when she wants it and darned well means to be let alone when she has other things on her mind'.[4] The protagonist of his *Silent Miaow: A Manual for Kittens, Strays, and Homeless Cats* (1964), purportedly written by Gallico's cat and illustrated with many attractive pictures of her, explains how, as a stray kitten, she spotted and took over a comfortable, prosperous home, even though its owners did not want a cat. She now controls them effortlessly: by making clear that cats are too independent to be expected to give affection, she can ensure that any bit she does bestow will be really appreciated; by adopting an irresistibly adorable pose, she can avoid being moved from their favourite chair.

Victorian-type sentimentality continues to appeal in stories and illustrations, and many dog lovers still cannot understand why anyone would bother with the self-contained, undeferential cat, but these attitudes are no longer predominant. Most of us would at least like to feel that we do not require unquestioning veneration and obedience from those who share our homes. By good-humouredly accepting feline determination to ignore our wishes, we can gratify our egalitarian feelings without really inconveniencing ourselves. We see our yielding as testimony to our liberal tolerance rather than exposure of our weakness in asserting mastery. In fact, we are rather proud of our discrimination in recognizing that cats have particular claims. The charge of cool self-centredness that in the past would have been a reproach to the cat has now become a tribute to its charm and our own tough-minded realism in accepting an animal that we know will never give us wholehearted devotion.

Although Jerome and Gallico endow cats with human articulateness, they retain authenticity by having them express convincingly feline feelings. In the same way, Angela Carter anthropomorphizes Puss in Boots in her witty retake on the traditional story, but she has clearly observed cats with insight and sympathy. Puss is still a poor man's servant, but, in accordance with the modern rise in cats' status, he is the valet-de-chambre of a dissolute young soldier and manifestly aware of his superior intellect. He tells his story himself, in artful prose that expresses his sophistication and worldly wisdom, as in his analysis of the difficulty of climbing up various types of building: a cat can easily move from cherub to wreath on a rococo façade, but it is nearly impossible to clamber up the plain Doric columns of a Palladian one. Puss helps his master feed the two of them (by stealing from the market), win at play (by moving from lap to lap at a card game or pouncing playfully on the dice to disrupt an unfortunate cast), and seduce women. When his master falls seriously in love with a rich old merchant's wife, whose jealous husband keeps her shut up, Puss sees that it is necessary to bring his mind back to business by curing him of his lovesickness; that is, by bringing them together in bed, which, in Puss's experience, is a sure cure for love. He makes friends with the merchant's tabby cat, who volunteers to fill the house with dead and dying rats, so they will have to call in the ratcatcher, who will of course be Puss's master in disguise, assisted by Puss. This brings them into the lady's bedroom, where Puss covers the lovers' amorous cries by noisily pursuing the rats. However, to Puss's disgust, his master continues to pine after the lady even after he has had her. So the two cats scheme again, Tabby trips the merchant on the stairs, his fall is fatal, and his fortune passes to his widow, who settles down happily with Puss's master and the two cats. Puss embodies the lustfulness, amorality and sly cleverness characteristic of cats with a human knowingness that might plausibly be attributed to them.[5]

A sophisticated, cultured, well-informed cat much like Puss is the narrator of a very widely read Japanese novel of the turn of the twentieth century, Natsume Soseki's *I Am a Cat*. Such a narrator is well suited to see through the intellectual pretensions that Soseki satirizes in his picture of middle class society. The (unnamed) cat belongs to Mr Kushami, a second-rate teacher of English in a junior high school, and has a certain fondness for him: 'Though he may be an idiot and an invalid, he is still my master . . . a cat sometimes feels sentimental about its master.' Because Kushami shuts himself up in his study every day, his family believes him to be very studious, as he does himself. But when the cat glides in to look, he finds him dozing over a book when he is not actually taking a nap. The cat reflects that he would not mind being reborn as a schoolteacher, because this job would not interfere with his sleeping as much as he likes. Nevertheless (like academics everywhere), Kushami is convinced that no job is so hard as teaching and constantly complains of overwork to his friends. Indeed, most humans display this absurd habit: 'whenever people get together, they commence telling each other how busy they are . . . They make such a fuss that you'd think they are killing themselves with overwork.' Even on the occasions when they really are busy, their activities are mostly unnecessary. 'Some humans express the wish to be as easy-going as I am. But if they want to be easy-going, all they have to do is to try . . . Nobody asked them to be so fussy.' At one point a wealthy businessman's wife invades Kushami's shabby home, confident that she can overawe him by mentioning her husband's position; but she makes no impression because Kushami is convinced that a junior high school teacher is far superior to any mere businessman, however rich. Through the cat's calm description, we see through the ludicrous self-importance of both parties.

While the cat shows the cool, critical self-possession that humans generally attribute to cats, he has certain distinctively Japanese characteristics. He believes he bears magic in his three-inch tail. More significantly, he is more conscientious than western cats, with a strong 'desire to serve justice and humanity'. And his life ends with an accident that suggests a Japanese ritual suicide. Feeling depressed by the conversation of his master and friends during a long beer drinking session, the cat drinks the leftover beer to feel better, gets drunk, falls into the rainbarrel and drowns; as he goes under, he feels he is entering 'the mysterious but wonderful realm of peace!'[6]

We not only tolerate and admire the cat's freedom, we envy it. Because we have not totally emancipated ourselves from Victorian inhibitions, we enjoy contemplating the freedom of an animal that acts out selfishness without hesitation or shame. As Robertson Davies wrote in *The Table Talk of Samuel Marchbanks*:

> The great charm of cats is their rampant egotism, their devil-may-care attitude toward responsibility, their disinclination to earn an honest dollar. In a continent which screams neurotically about cooperation and the Golden Rule, cats are disdainful of everything but their own immediate interests and they contrive to be so suave and delightful about it that they even receive the apotheosis of a National Cat Week.

In Saki's (H. H. Munro's) 'Tobermory,' a tomcat who has been taught to talk coolly voices his thoughts and feelings while the human guests at a house party, constrained to conceal them in order to preserve propriety, babble in helpless embarrassment. Only the cat can be comfortable, because only he is unashamed of himself and his actions.[7]

Several short stories are based on the comic contrast between the freedom of cats and the restrictions that constrain humans.

The protagonist of Theodore Sturgeon's sardonic tale 'Fluffy' (1947) is a human with a cat's values. Ransome is a charming parasite, a perpetual houseguest who lives off hosts he despises. Currently staying with a fatuous woman, he hates her pampered cat, Fluffy, for succeeding even better than he does in being loved, despite their common failings of selfishness, ingratitude, cold-heartedness and insincerity. As Ransome thinks how intolerably irritating his hostess is, Fluffy informs him that he feels the same way and has throttled her in her sleep. Then he gracefully skips out and leaves Ransome to bear the responsibility – only a cat can make his way with charm alone. In Roy Vickers's 'Miss Paisley's Cat' (1953), identification with a cat liberates a woman crippled by her genteel inhibitions. Miss Paisley, a lady in reduced circumstances who is exploited and snickered at by the more effectual people around her, takes in a bold, ugly cat and soon comes to love him. Under his influence, she finds the courage to assert her wishes and confront vulgar people. Horrified at first when she sees him playing with a mouse, she becomes interested herself and comes to share in his pleasure. Finally, when her brutish neighbour hangs the cat, she is not only able to murder him to avenge it, but to do so with feline efficiency and satisfaction. In Ann Chadwick's 'Smith', a poverty-stricken avant-garde writer turns into an equally shabby ginger tomcat. As a cat, he is free of the aesthetic standards that limited his popularity as a human writer; and he dictates extremely successful cheap romances. He develops self-confidence and expands into an attractive character.[8] Imagining ourselves as cats, we can imagine ourselves free of impractical aspirations, moral inhibitions and social pressures to conform.

Artists may use feline independence to symbolize the element in humans that is immune to outside influences. In 'The Cat', Baudelaire visualized his inner self, the part of his mind that was authentic because unsocialized, as a cat prowling through his brain as if it owned the place. Both the cat and the inner self, from which poetic inspiration comes, are uncontrollable and impervious to social pressures. Joyce Carol Oates spelled out this connection in an introduction written in 1992: because cats are wild and unreachable under their 'seemingly civilized ways', they appeal to the artist's 'unknowable and unpredictable core of being which . . . we designate "the imagination" or "the unconscious."'[9]

In *Kitty Libber: Cat Cartoons by Women* (1992), where equality between women and their cat friends is assumed, many of the cartoons turn on comic, yet plausible, role reversals between cats and women. Andrea Natalie's 'Tabby dreams she takes Louise to get fixed' shows four cat surgeons operating on a woman while one says, 'There! Now she won't always be whining every time she doesn't have a lover.' Roberta Gregory's Muffy is depressed because she has been yelled at for clawing the stereo speaker. She tries to make amends by presenting her owner with a nice gift of a dead mouse, left on her pillow so 'she'll know it's just for *her*'. When the plan backfires, her friend Smudge wonders, 'Sometimes these humans can be *darn* near impossible to figure out . . .'

Another consequence of the new equality is the greater frequency with which cats appear as friends of men. On greeting cards before the 1980s, cats were never shown with or used to represent males of any age. Now they appear with men as often as with women. In the past, an ordinary, conventional young man like Jon in Jim Davis's comic strip *Garfield* would have been paired with a dog. Now it is Garfield the cat who is his closest friend. Jon approaches his front door wistfully telling himself, 'Bachelorhood is OK, I guess', and then continues in the next frame, 'But you just can't beat . . .' and then, as Garfield runs joyfully to greet him: 'Someone waiting for you when you get home.'

Garfield is a typical cat in his love of comfort, his choosiness, his readiness to steal food, his skilful manipulation of Jon and the artless dog, Odie, and his calm refusal to look up to Jon or defer to his wishes. In one recent strip (27 June 2005), Garfield smilingly introduces 'Man's Best Friend'. Odie appears, grinning and slobbering with enthusiasm. In the final panel, Garfield comments, 'Better you than me.' However, the strip would be wittier if Garfield were consistently a cat; Davis has gone too far in making him one of the boys. Garfield is entirely human when he can't wait to open his Christmas presents or pigs out on chocolate chip cookies or sits in front of the television set and clicks the channel changer because he has a short attention span. (In fact, cats are particularly notable for their quiet, relentless persistence.) Although Garfield is not sentimentalized, he is as anthropomorphic as Louis Wain's cute kittens. He fills the traditional animal role of symbolizing the self-indulgent appetites that humans do not like to recognize in themselves, though Davis presents with amused tolerance what medieval preachers castigated as greed and sloth.

Jon's primary attachment to a cat might simply indicate that men have become more relaxed about gender roles. But we now find similar attachments in men who make a point of their virility. In Robert A. Heinlein's *The Door into Summer*, the best friend of the rugged individualist narrator is his tomcat, Petronius the Arbiter, who is even more obviously virile than he is. The man's treacherous fiancée first reveals her vile nature by her attitude toward Pete. She dislikes him, although she pretends otherwise; and, even worse, she proposes having him castrated for convenience. The hero is horrified at the idea of making 'a eunuch of that old warrior' and changing 'him into a fireside decoration',

Promotion poster for the United States Tank Corps, 1917, lithograph: a rare example of the cat as an emblem of virility.

and goes on to suggest sarcastically that she have him castrated as well: 'I'd be much more docile and I'd stay home nights and I'd never argue with you.' The man not only identifies with his cat, but projects onto him the full symbolic significance that male genitals have to men. J. D. MacDonald, author of the detective series featuring the virile Travis McGee, originally sneered at cats as pets for women and gays, but later credited them with helping him to learn to write. He interprets their 'sporadic demonstrations of affection in return for their demanded measure of household equality' and 'their conservative insistence on

order, habit, and routine' as manifestations of masculine independence and discipline that promote prolonged creative effort
more effectively than 'doggy devotion'.[10]

The idea of admiring cats for manly self-discipline goes back
much further in Japan. In the traditional story of the *neko-myo-
jutsu*, the master cat, a samurai was plagued by a monster rat
that rampaged through his house even in broad daylight. His
own cat fled shrieking before it, as did the bravest and most skilful cats in the neighbourhood. He himself tried to kill it, but the
rat effortlessly dodged his sword. Finally he brought in an old cat
known for its mysterious powers as a hunter. He looked like an
ordinary cat and appeared entirely unconcerned, sitting serenely while the rat came in and made fun of him. Then he slowly got
up, coolly seized the rat by the neck, and dispatched it. At the
request of the samurai and the other cats, the hero explained his
principles, based mainly on self-control: take time to study your
adversary and put him off guard by appearing inoffensive, and
only then, pounce, fight and conquer. A cat's control of its movements, patience in observing its prey and bravery made it a good
model for a samurai warrior.[11] A popular television programme
in Japan featured a samurai nicknamed 'Sleeping Cat'.

Cats are not models, but simply pleasant companions in the
contemporary novels of Haruki Murakami; indeed, they clearly
fill the role of man's best friend. In *The Wind-Up Bird Chronicle*,
Toru Okada's orderly life unravels when his cat disappears and
begins to reintegrate when it comes back. Petting the cat gives
him unqualified pleasure, which is lacking in his numerous
bizarre sexual encounters with women: 'I had not thought about
the cat's special, soft, warm touch for a very long time . . .
Holding this soft, small living creature in my lap this way . . .
and seeing how it slept with complete trust in me, I felt a warm
rush in my chest.' Coming home the following night, 'I took the

cat on my knees and confirmed his warmth and softness with my hands. Having spent the day in separate places, we both confirmed the fact that we were home.'

When Kafka Tamura, the alienated fifteen-year-old protagonist of *Kafka on the Shore*, meets a cat, he naturally stops to pet it; the animal 'narrows his eyes and starts to purr', and 'We sit there on the stairs for a long time, each enjoying his own version of this intimate feeling.' Nakata, the amiable brain-damaged old man who is in some way Kafka's counterpart, makes his initial appearance talking with a cat as if this were perfectly ordinary. He has been able to do this ever since he lost his ability to read and other conventional human learning. Cats are now the only friends who understand him and with whom he never runs out of subjects for conversation, and they help him in his occupation of locating lost cats. He treats them with politeness and respect, and they point out that someone who can talk with cats cannot be as stupid as people say. He converses with a variety of cats, from the stray tabby Kawamura, also brain-damaged, to the clever, sophisticated Siamese Mimi, who explains that her owner, an opera lover, named her for the character in *La Bohème*. When Nakata apologetically explains that he assigns names to unowned cats because humans need names and dates to remember things by, an elderly black tomcat scoffs that this sounds like a pain; cats don't need names because, 'We go by smell, shape, things of this nature.' Nakata and the cats share a taste for eel, although the old tomcat has had it only once, a long time ago, and Mimi points out that you couldn't eat it all the time.[12] These conversations seem totally natural, without self-consciousness or artfulness on either side. The cats sound authentically catlike – self-contained, cool, matter-of-fact, forthright and, unless they have been traumatized by awful experiences, well-disposed toward humans. Despite their articulateness, they add a refreshing realistic element to the surreal atmosphere and bizarre human motivation in *Kafka* and Murakami's other novels.

Although stereotypes still remain – both old ones like the cat as sweet innocuous pet and the cat as cute child, and new ones like the cat as smart aleck – it does seem that today we are more ready to understand cats and to respect them for what they are. As a result, in memoirs and realistic fiction as well, cats' personalities are analysed, and cat–human relationships may be presented as friendships between equals. Many stories in Michael J. Rosen's significantly titled 1992 anthology *The Company of Cats* present without criticism central characters whose most satisfactory social relationship is with a cat.

Victorian Chattie and Jacobina were loved and valued, but they remained pets, and the humans who were most attached to them were disparaged for their attachment. Cats in twentieth-century stories can reinforce their owners' personalities and situations without any hint of patronage. Radclyffe Hall's 'Fräulein Schwartz' (1934) and Doris Lessing's 'An Old Woman and Her Cat' (1972) develop the traditional association between cats and poor, outcast old women, but show with a new perceptiveness how people and cats can share qualities and the problems these produce. Fräulein Schwartz, a solitary, gentle German woman living in a London boarding-house, takes in a stray cat and lavishes all her love upon him. During the bitterness of World War I, her neighbours turn against her and finally vent their hatred by poisoning her cat. Cat and woman are equally innocent, equally inoffensive, equally incapable of dealing with the world's hostility.

Doris Lessing's story wins sympathy for a less amiable couple. Hetty, a rag-trader who would rather live on the streets than submit to the regulations of an old people's home, cherishes a battered tomcat as her only friend. They are equally indifferent to cleanliness and respectability, law and order. After Hetty dies of exposure while hiding from the authorities that would regulate her life, the cat is caught and 'put to sleep'. An orderly society has disposed of two undesirable members, yet the reader is left with the conviction that there should be a better way of dealing with nonconformists. Both stories plausibly use cats to reinforce and clarify their person's inevitable victimization by an unsympathetic society, whether she is a defenseless scapegoat like Fräulein Schwartz or an incorrigible nonconformist like Hetty.[13]

May Sarton's biography of her cat Tom Jones, *The Fur Person*, describes his maturation into a social cat from his own point of view and presents their relationship as a credit to both of them. Tom Jones, who started as a stray with no attachments to humans, ultimately 'has given up part of his cat self into human keeping'. Therefore, he is at the same time 'the ineffable Mr Jones walking down the street, greeting man and cat with equal dignity' and 'an anxious tender personality who followed the two Voices [his human guardians] up and down the stairs and round the house, begging for a lap'. He comes to recognize himself as 'a Fur Person', that is, 'a cat who is also a person': at the same time that he loves humans and is loved by them, they allow him to keep 'his dignity, his reserve, and his freedom'. 'This can only happen if the human being has imagined part of himself into a cat . . . just as the cat has imagined part of himself into a human being.'[14]

Because we can now accept animals as quasi-equal beings whose feelings and claims can be presented as important without being falsely inflated into human ones, fiction writers have become able to create a cat's consciousness that seems free of projected human values. The seventeenth-century French aristocrats who wrote love letters in their cats' names did not make a serious effort to imagine what cats might possibly feel: rather, by putting human sentiments into feline mouths, they drew attention to the comic disparity between human and cat and thus used their cats to show off their own wit. Two centuries later, Louise Patteson's *Pussy Meow: The Autobiography of a Cat* (1901) was genuinely inspired by a desire to promote proper care for cats and to make clear the evil of abandoning them. However, Patteson justified her claims by practically making them into dogs. It is important, for example, to give a cat a name, so that he will develop 'a sense of dignity and self-respect' and 'a chance to exercise promptness and obedience', because he knows it is he who is wanted and 'can get right up and run'. Along with her suspiciously canine desire to be 'a good and useful cat',[15] Pussy has the sexual innocence of a nineteenth-century young lady: she cannot understand how six kittens have got into her basket, since it is too early for Santa Claus's visit. Fortunately, like the ideal Victorian mother, she instinctively knows just how to take care of them.

Beverley Cleary's *Socks* (1973), on the other hand, convincingly renders the family cat's point of view and concerns on the arrival of a baby: Cleary presents his natural hostility with honesty and understanding. Socks resents being displaced from the centre of his owners' affection, although he is partly consoled by snacks of leftover formula milk. He gets pitched out the door when he clamours for attention at the same time that the three human members of the family are demanding that their needs be met. Ultimately he learns that he can share pleasurably in the baby's mischief-making and sleep in his crib. Although it teaches a nineteenth-century type moral of overcoming selfishness, with a lesson that could apply to an elder sibling as well as the household cat, it is made authentic by truth to nature and sympathetic understanding.

In *Blitzcat*, Robert Westall successfully represented wartime Britain through a cat's consciousness, while strongly engaging our interest in her welfare and the success of her quest. He traces the cat's journey home across England during World War II and her encounters with people along the way. He enlists sympathy for her, but he does not sentimentalize her; she is no more than mildly attached to humans she knows and finds congenial. She leaves the new home she dislikes for her old home, where she expects to find her favourite human, not knowing he is away with the RAF:

It is impossible to understand exactly what was on her mind. But she was used to having her own way. She did not like noise and upset. She hated the strange house at Beamister, full of women and children, tears and tantrums. She hated the smells of sour milk and nappies, and the toddlers in every room who would not leave her in peace . . . and she hated the way her own people no longer had any time to stroke and fuss her. She hated the kitchen scraps she was fed, instead of fresh-boiled fish . . . She was going back to where she'd been peaceful; where she could spend hours alone, sleeping on the silken coverlet of a sunlit bed in the long afternoons; where she could go to the kitchen and get fresh fish and milk on demand.[16]

She stays with a series of people and helps all of them, although Westall never resorts to far-fetched circumstance or unfeline altruism. She moves with her kitten into the woodshed of a war widow simply because it is the most convenient shelter. Although the widow has withdrawn into depression and does not want to bother with them, she cannot let them starve on her premises and caring for them pulls her out of her selfish apathy. At the end, however, there is a shocking ironic twist: when the cat finally succeeds in her quest, it appears that her devotion and persistence will be casually thrown away. Her travels have taken her to Europe on a fighter plane, and her man has no scruples about killing her in order to comply with rabies quarantine regulations. This obliviousness to the hero's aims and efforts is a quiet but telling comment on human callousness toward animals, which persists despite our advances in understanding and considering them. Westall's convincing rendition of a cat's consciousness forces us to recognize her rights and feelings as an independent being.

6 The Fascination of Paradox

In late seventeenth-century France, the idea that cats could be valued companions was a new fashion among an aristocratic coterie; now it is an obvious assumption among all classes of society. There are dissenting opinions, of course. Some dog lovers simply cannot understand why anyone would keep a cat when they could have a dog instead. Some bird lovers condemn cats for killing birds and become actually vituperative in their denunciations of feline bloodthirstiness. Typically these moralists overestimate the bird mortality, and always they forget that predation is nature's way. Rodents, who can suffer at least as much as birds, fail to evoke the same sympathy. Rats and mice, of course, unlike songbirds, have historically been seriously destructive of human property. Even today, some cats earn their keep catching rodent pests on farms, where they are often considered workers rather than pets.

But the main utilitarian purpose to which cats are put nowadays is as experimental subjects in laboratories. They are still, as they have always been, widely available and cheap. Dead cats are commonly used for dissection in schools and colleges and have been at least since 1881, when St George Mivart published his textbook, *The Cat: An Introduction to the Study of Backboned Animals, Especially Mammals*. Live cats are now used chiefly for limited, specialized research. They are larger than rats and

Swiss School, *The Cat and the Goldfinches*, early 19th century.

smaller and easier to keep than dogs. As researcher Kristina Narfstrom explains, 'Dogs need to be walked on a daily basis to be happy while cats are quite content if they have large spacious cages, are kept together in groups and have things to play with.' Since both species require daily socialization, she brings in students to play with her cat colony.

Some of the research on cats has benefited their own species, leading to improvements in diagnostic and surgical techniques, treatments for diabetes and arthritis, and development of vaccines. Other research promotes the welfare of their endangered wild relatives, whose problems are aggravated by infertility and inbreeding. Scientists at the National Zoo in Washington are using oocytes from domestic cats to work out the best procedure to preserve feline egg cells by freezing them in liquid nitrogen, so that it will be possible to thaw them several years later, fertilize them in vitro and implant the embryos in another cat's uterus. Once the technique is developed, it can be used to facilitate reproduction in wild species such as cheetahs. This research does not harm its cat subjects at all, for the investigators use ovaries obtained from spay clinics.

However, most research on cats is undertaken to learn about human anatomy and the treatment of human disease. Eight Nobel prizes in physiology have been awarded for research on cats that elucidated the structure of the human nervous system. David H. Hubel and Torsten N. Wiesel won the prize in 1981 for mapping the complex pathways that transmit messages from the light-sensitive cells in the retina to the primary visual cortex in the brain. This knowledge has led to the discovery of a treatment for strabismus, cross-eye. Hubel and Wiesel also discovered that if visual stimuli are blocked during a certain early critical period, these pathways fail to develop and there will be permanent visual impairment in cats or humans. Narfstrom is investigating the effectiveness of retinal transplantations and stem cell therapy on Abyssinian cats with a photoreceptor disorder that is hereditary in this breed and closely resembles the human retinal blinding disease retinitis pigmentosa. The cat is the preferred model for research on the visual system because it has bifocal vision, like humans, and its large eyes approximate the size of human eyes. For this reason, it can be used to develop surgical techniques and instrumentation to improve ophthalmic operations on humans. The researchers on cats have amassed an invaluable database for analogous studies on the human nervous system.

Cats have certain inherited and immunodeficiency diseases that are sufficiently similar to analogous diseases in humans that cats can serve as useful models for investigating the genetic origins, progress and treatment of these human diseases. Feline immunodeficiency virus (FIV) is close enough to human

AIDS that studies of the effects of FIV on cats can clarify similar effects produced by AIDS in humans, and vaccines developed for FIV may be adapted to HIV. Moreover, because infected cats generally resist the symptoms of FIV better than humans do those of HIV, studying the feline immune system could lead to discoveries that would help the human immune system to control HIV. Because experimenters can deliberately induce the disease in cats, as they cannot in humans, they can use cats to analyse its progress in detail in conditions where the nature and timing of the infection are carefully controlled. Inherited diseases are easier to study in cats than humans because cats reproduce so quickly. One investigator is examining cat foetuses collected by caesarian operations at different stages of development in order to better understand mother-to-infant transmission of HIV. Another plans to inject cats with the FIV virus at birth, at eight weeks old, and as adults 'to compare the serial immunodeficiency and neurologic impairment'.[1]

Unfortunately, however, not all feline suffering in the laboratory can be justified by a reasonable expectation that it will help humans or even produce useful knowledge. When investigators at Yale University in 1954 subjected kittens to repeated overheating, causing repeated convulsions, they learned that overheating produced the same symptoms as it had in human beings and in previous batches of kittens. In 1972 some investigators at Brown University compressed the testicles of tomcats to find out whether the results would be the same as in men; sure enough, the cats produced 'a painlike response'. In the same year, two scientists at Florida State University, who recognized the cat's 'reputation as a difficult behavioral subject' but wanted to use this 'organism' so 'extremely interesting . . . for sensory experiments', proudly reported that they had devised a technique that eliminated their feline subjects' resistance; it consisted of food deprivation and constant electric shocks.[2] Such experimentation will occur as long as investigators are allowed to determine for themselves what procedures are warranted on animal subjects.

On the other hand, the public's affection for their pets and increasing concern for animals' rights has stimulated serious protests against research on cats, as well as dogs. The nineteenth-century Cartesian Claude Bernard dissected both animals without inhibition, insisting that a howling, struggling cat was no more than a machine and that placing its pain before the advancement of science was mawkish sentimentality. Researchers now acknowledge that it is desirable to reduce the number of animals used in experiments, replacing them with other models whenever possible, and to make an effort to treat them as humanely as the requirements of the experiment permit. It is now understood that well cared for animals, living in an environment relatively free of stress, provide the most reliable research results. The number of animal subjects has been reduced in the case of cats and dogs, who together comprise less than 0.5 per cent of the laboratory animals used in the United States and the United Kingdom.

At present, for the first time in history, cats widely rival dogs as the pet of first choice. In 1980 there were more than twice as many owned dogs than owned cats in the United Kingdom but by 1995 cats outnumbered dogs by over 400,000. The figures for 2002, the latest available, are about 7,500,000 cats kept as companions and 6,100,000 dogs. Comparable figures for the United States are 53,831,000 dogs and 44,579,000 cats in 1981, and 78,038,000 cats to only 61,278,000 dogs in 2003.[3] Of course there are practical reasons – cats are better suited than dogs to living in small apartments where no one is at home all day. But mostly it is because we have finally recognized that cats can be agreeable members of the family.

Far from feeling any need to defend their choice of a cat as a companion, contemporary cat lovers plume themselves on their preference. The distinguished historian A. L. Rowse made a book out of his devotion to his cat, Peter. He tells the world every detail about Peter, from his fondness for sponge cake crumbs to the baby-talk endearments that Rowse used to coo in his ear. He complains of his trials with foolish women who courted him by professing interest in his cat, 'as if I didn't care infinitely more for him than for them'.[4] Cleveland Amory got three 250-page bestsellers out of his pet Polar Bear, *The Cat Who Came for Christmas* (1987), *The Cat and the Curmudgeon* (1990) and *The Best Cat Ever* (1993). Along with some amusing anecdotes and accurate observations, there are chapters of self-indulgent padding (how to name a cat, what astrological sign would fit Polar Bear) and many tales of cute curmudgeonry based on the assumption that the refusal to obey or cooperate is particularly endearing. Anyone who fails to appreciate Polar Bear's adorably cute behaviour must be a clod or a poor sport.

The first book to be devoted entirely to cats was François-Augustin Paradis de Moncrif's *History of Cats* (1727). Half serious research and advocacy, half *jeu d'esprit*, the work describes cat worship in ancient Egypt, defends cats against the common charges that they are antisocial and treacherous and assist witches, and praises their independence, playfulness and elegant poses. However, de Moncrif felt it necessary to protect himself from charges of fatuity by advancing burlesque arguments, praising the music of feline voices and narrating with mock refinement a tragic romance that ended when an unsympathetic neighbour made the tomcat into 'a new Atys'. Even so, contemporary reactions demonstrated that he did not protect himself sufficiently for an age that still, for the most part, dismissed cats as insignificant animals kept only because they were useful. Although his work proved very popular, it seriously jeopardized his reputation as an intellectual and man of letters.

While de Moncrif's light-minded book had elicited ridicule that was to haunt him throughout his career, Champfleury's (Jules Husson's) serious and rather vacuous *Cats* of 1868 won a fame it did not deserve, presumably because its time had come. His English contemporary Charles Henry Ross felt he was taking a risk when he published a book about cats, but his *Feline Facts and Fancies* was enthusiastically received.

Now it seems that the word *cat* can sell almost any book. There are *The Jewish Cat Book* (1983), *French for Cats* (1992) and several feline astrology books that gravely analyse the personalities of the Aries cat and so forth through the Zodiac. It seems that half the detectives in fiction are inspired by one or two pet cats. Lilian Jackson Braun sells many books by titling them *The Cat Who...* and featuring a virile detective who dotes on his two mischievous Siamese, whose adorably cute actions are retailed at length. Even the ancient Roman detective in Steven Saylor's *Roman Blood* (1991) has a cat, the pet of his Egyptian slave. In Japan, too, cats are featured in popular detective stories, such as Niki Etsuko's *Nekowa shitte ita* (*The Cat Knew*, 1957) and Akagawa Jiro's *Mikeneko Homozu no suiri* (*The Deductions of Calico Cat Holmes*, 1978).

The Clintons' Socks was not the first White House cat, but he was the first to be a public figure, regularly appearing in political cartoons and in the celebrity-doings column of the *Washington Post*. (Significantly, perhaps, no cat is prominent in the current Republican administration.) *Cats* (1981), an empty show blown up from nonsense verses T. S. Eliot tossed off for a friend's children, was a sensational success. Jim Davis's pudgy

Cartoon in the
Washington Post,
8 December 1994:
beset by political
crises, President
Bill Clinton suffers
a final, devastating
blow – desertion
by his cat.

Garfield appears daily in 1,300 newspapers and is the centre of
a multimillion-dollar industry that includes books, T-shirts,
mugs and greeting cards. Currently the comics pages of the
Washington Post include five strips about households with a cat
and a dog, in which the cat typically displays superior sophistication and dominance – *Get Fuzzy*, *Pickles*, *Mother Goose and
Grimm*, *Mutts* and *Garfield*. In addition, the grown daughter in
For Better or Worse has just brought home the cat she adopted
and is introducing her to the family dogs. Chronically wrong-
headed young Nate in *Big Nate* recurrently makes himself ridiculous by jeering at his friend's cat. And in *Sally Forth* the Forth
parents have given up a long-anticipated trip to Paris because
Kitty required a $3,400 operation and they could not bear to

devastate their daughter, who never doubted that Kitty was worth any amount of money.

Cats were welcomed into film from the beginning. Felix the Cat, a resourceful 'little man' in the tradition of Tybert in *Reynard the Fox*, was one of the earliest stars of animated cartoons, appearing about 1914. He was displaced, however, by Walt Disney's Mickey Mouse, and the predominance of this mouse hero set a tone of hostility to cats in animated films. Hanna Barbera's *Tom and Jerry* cartoons of the 1930s and 1940s are actually sadistic. Jerry always outwits the bully Tom, who typically ends up flattened or toothless. However, the hero of Disney's late movie *The Aristocats* (1970) is an elegant white mother cat who flees with her kittens from a scheming butler and is rescued by an exuberant tomcat named O'Malley. The creators of *Shrek 2* (2004) wisely introduced an engaging Puss in

A scene from Andrew Lloyd Webber's musical *Cats* (1981).

Advertisement for Dubonnet, c. 1895.

Souvenir programme for the Chat-Noir Cabaret in Paris, c. 1915.

Boots to enhance the appeal of this sequel that they hoped would equal its highly successful original.

Cats have been used in live-action pictures as much as possible, considering their reluctance to cooperate. When a stray gray cat climbed through a broken floorboard onto the set of a Mike Sennett comedy in the 1920s, the director immediately saw the advantage of including her in the action. The actress pouring cream for coffee deliberately spilled some, and the cat cautiously sniffed at the cream and dipped her paw in. The scene was a big success and Pepper, as the cat was named, starred in many other films, sometimes in amicable companionship with a white

Advertisement for International Baking Powder, c. 1885, which makes dough rise so powerfully that it elevates an agitated cat.

Advertisement for Ethyl Gasoline, 1929–31: 'to make your engine purr'.

First appearing in 1933, the kitten Chessie demonstrated the comfort of the Chesapeake and Ohio Railroad's sleeping cars for many years.

TO MAKE YOUR ENGINE PURR...USE ETHYL

mouse. Cats continue to enhance movies, as witches' familiars in *Bedknobs and Broomsticks* (1971) and *Bell, Book, and Candle* (1958), as close friends of the unconventional heroine in *Breakfast at Tiffany's* (1961) and the intrepid commanding officer of the doomed space ship in *Alien* (1979), and even as the centre of a comic fantasy, when a cat inherits a baseball team in *Rhubarb* (1951). Directors, however, have to make the most of natural feline behaviour such as prowling, snarling or cuddling in a human's arms. Orangey, a large, chunky ginger tomcat, won awards for his performances in *Rhubarb* and *Breakfast at Tiffany's*, but all he did was allow himself to be picked up and held, jump up or down on people's shoulders, perch on high shelves and alertly follow moving objects with his eyes.

Sometimes, however, a cat's natural behaviour can be used to produce a highly effective scene. Marlon Brando's prolonged caressing of a cat in *The Godfather* (1972) wonderfully enhances his aura of sinister, understated power; man and cat reinforce each other's cool superiority to the petitioners who come before them. There is a terrifying sequence in *The Incredible Shrinking Man* (1957) where the hero, reduced to two inches high, is stalked by the family cat. (The feline actor was actually inspired by a bird kept just beyond reach.) But in general, the use of cats in horror films is disappointing. The diabolically resuscitated Churchill in *Pet Sematary* (1989) is a perfectly ordinary disagreeable cat. In *Strays* (1991) a demon tomcat leads a pack of cats to murder humans, but there is no attempt to make their behaviour plausible or to exploit the genuinely terrifying potentialities of feline lurking, stalking and pouncing.

Whether we measure in terms of popular fashion or loving companionship, cats today are more widely liked than ever before. Yet they have always fascinated humans by the seem-

Marlon Brando in *The Godfather* (1972).

The hero of *The Incredible Shrinking Man* (1957), reduced to two inches tall and living in a doll's house, is hunted by his family cat, now a terrifying predator.

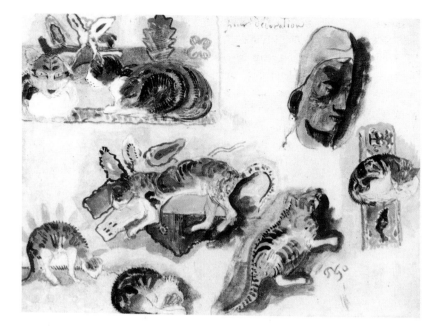

Paradoxical cat
behaviour in Paul
Gauguin's water-
colour sketch of
c. 1897, *Study of
Cats and a Head*.

ingly contradictory impressions they produce. At any time, the soft, pretty pet can turn into a miniature tiger. The cat that appears so benign as it smilingly relaxes on the sofa will mobilize instantly if a small animal appears and demonstrate the superb senses and muscular coordination of wild relatives that hunt for their living. If threatened, it turns into a formidable fighter with flailing limbs, bristling hair, long extended claws and gaping jaws full of teeth. The visual characterization of Puss in Boots in *Shrek 2*, called in to kill the ogre Shrek because he had demonstrated his capacity for ogre-killing in Perrault's tale, captures these instant changes. Puss is an ostentatiously fierce swashbuckler, yet when it does not suit him to fight, he can instantly melt any opponent by gazing at him. No one can resist a steady, confiding gaze from large eyes that seem to consist entirely of warmly dark, liquid pupils.

While an embattled cat is genuinely alarming, a cat in peaceful repose actually soothes our spirit. Feline calm and harmony are beyond the reach of humans, but we can feel them for a time as we contemplate the cat in our home. As Smart wrote of his beloved Geoffry, 'there is nothing brisker than his life when in motion' and 'nothing sweeter than his peace when at rest'. In *Pudd'n-head Wilson* Mark Twain described an idyllic American village composed of whitewashed frame houses adorned with flowery window boxes and a cat –

> stretched at full length, asleep and blissful, with her furry belly to the sun and a paw curved over her nose. Then that house was complete, and its contentment and peace were made manifest to the world by this symbol, whose testimony is infallible. A home without a cat – and a well-fed, well-petted, and properly revered cat – may be a perfect home, perhaps, but can it prove title?'

Théophile-Alexandre Steinlen's sketch of a mother cat and kitten.

Théophile-Alexandre Steinlen's engaging drawing of *The Cat and the Frog*, 1884.

(It is true that there may be a hint of irony here, since the villagers are provincial hypocrites whose prosperity is founded on slavery. On the other hand, cats do not have to concern themselves with moral issues.) The exuberant leaps and pounces of a playful cat enliven our spirits as much as the peace of a placid one soothes them. As Joanna Baillie rightly claimed, the wild yet graceful mock ferocity of a kitten enchants everyone from a tired peasant to a scholar, from a depressed lonely widow to a determined misanthropist.[5]

The elegant, poised animal who seems born to grace the parlour is equally at home prowling around cellars and gutters. The model of serene dignity is just as truly a sly little predator, ever ready to snag a bit of fish. Cats are so beautiful, graceful and reserved that we see them as more elegant and fastidious than humans, and admirers like Rowse and Colette's Alain can plume themselves on their discrimination in preferring cats to women. Colette herself had made the same mistake of attributing human sensibilities to her cat, and she comically described her disillusionment. She takes her 'She-Shah', an elegant, pampered blue Persian cat, to a country house swarming with rough workmen and is distraught when the cat disappears: surely the workmen will terrify her. But when at last the cat is found, she is sitting in the middle of a circle of dirty workmen eating their lunch:

> there, smiling and very much at home, with her tail upright and her whiskers curling, in the midst of a din of oaths and coarse laughter, is the She-Shah, the divine She-Shah, gorged with cheese-rinds, rancid bacon and sausage skins, purring, spinning round after her tail, and playing to the gallery of masons.[6]

The neat, demure cat, who seems so much more quiet and orderly than the boisterous dog, pays no attention to human rules and thus enjoys a freedom beyond reach of dogs or humans. The companion who seems so cuddly, congenial, and friendly can at other times seem to withdraw into a world of its own, unfathomable to humans. Although they live in our homes, share our comforts and enjoy our company, cats have retained their wildness more than any other domesticated animal. As Michael Hamburger wrote of his 'delicately tough' 'London Tom-Cat', 'He conjures tangled forests in a furnished flat.'[7]

The paradoxically diverse images that cats present, together with the incongruity that they are so close to us and at the same time so detached by their independence and reserve, have inspired authors and artists to wonderfully inventive imaginative creations. Because dogs, the other animals that live with us, want to be as close to us as possible and show us all their feelings, we think of them as junior people; they do not elicit the fascination that cats do, and the best portrayals of dogs in literature are realistic rather than fantastic or symbolic. But a cat can be a gentle little pet, like Fräulein Schwartz's Karl Heinrich; an elegant aristocrat, like Mme d'Aulnoy's White Cat; a clever trickster, like Puss in Boots; the tough comrade of a virile man, like Heinlein's Petronius; a cold-blooded killer, like Sturgeon's Fluffy; a plump sybarite, like Garfield; a model of self-assured coolness, like Saki's Tobermory; or a bearer of mysterious powers, whether he brings exciting adventure like Dr Seuss's Cat in the Hat or inexorable vengeance like Poe's Black Cat.

Pierre-Auguste Renoir, *Geraniums and Cats*, 1881, oil on canvas.

Timeline of the Cat

c. 2 million years ago	Before 2000 BC	*c.* 1450 BC	*c.* 950 BC
Felis sylvestris, ancestor of domestic cat, splits off from other cat lineages	Cat is domesticated in Egypt; its name, *miw*, is first recorded	Cat appears regularly in Egyptian paintings on tomb walls	Local cat goddess, Bastet, rises to national prominence in Egypt

500	9th century	10th century	1558	1620
Cat appears in Indian *Pancatantra*	'Pangur Ban', first recorded expression of affection for a cat	Laws of Welsh King Hywel Dda codify monetary value of cats, based on their value as mouse catchers	Cats were burned alive in an effigy of the pope in Queen Elizabeth's coronation procession	Pilgrims brought first domestic cats to America on the *Mayflower*

1879–80	1871	1895	1899	1906
When the original design for the Queen's Medal for Kindness of the RSPCA failed to include a cat, Queen Victoria draws one in with her own hand	First cat show staged, at the Crystal Palace in London	First cat show in America, in Madison Square Garden, New York	Veblen approves of cats because they are not suitable vehicles for conspicuous consumption	Cat Fanciers' Association is formed in US

5th century BC	4th century BC	200 BC – AD 200	AD 350	4th century AD
Herodotus reports on domesticated cats in Egypt	Aristotle remarks on lechery of female cats	Cats were probably introduced into China	Word *catus* first appears, in Palladius' treatise on agriculture	Domestic cats have reached England

1713	1727	1749–67	1821	1832
Alexander Pope protests cruelty to cats in a *Guardian* essay	Paradis de Moncrif's *History of Cats*, the first book on cats	Buffon denounces the cat's moral character in his *Natural History*	A proposed law to prevent the abuse of horses is laughed down in Parliament when a member facetiously proposes that it be extended to protect cats	Cat appears as a prominent character in a novel, Bulwer-Lytton's *Eugene Aram*

1910	1916	1981	1993	1995
Governing Council of the Cat Fancy unites cat clubs of Britain	Edward Howe Forbush, state ornithologist of Massachusetts, denounces cats as ferocious bird-killers in an official report	*Cats*, a musical based on Eliot's *Old Possum's Book of Practical Cats*, is a sensational success	Pet cats outnumber pet dogs for the first time in the US	Pet cats outnumber pet dogs for the first time in the UK

References

1 WILDCAT TO DOMESTIC MOUSECATCHER

1 Robert Darnton, *The Great Cat Massacre and Other Episodes in French Cultural History* (New York, 1985), p. 103.
2 David Alderton, *Wild Cats of the World* (New York, 1998), pp. 78, 84–5; Alan Turner, *The Big Cats and Their Fossil Relatives: An Illustrated Guide to Their Evolution and Natural History* (New York, 1997), pp. 25–6, 30, 34, 36, 99, 106; R. F. Ewer, *The Carnivores* (Ithaca, NY, 1973), pp. 360–61, 374, 375.
3 John Seidensticker and Susan Lumpkin, *Cats: Smithsonian Answer Book* (Washington, DC, 2004), pp. 8, 15, 17, 20–21, 131–3; Ewer, *Carnivores*, p. 57; Paul Leyhausen in *Grzimek's Encyclopedia of Mammals* (New York, 1990), vol. III, pp. 576, 580.
4 Roger Tabor, *The Wildlife of the Domestic Cat* (London, 1983), p. 191; Seidensticker and Lumpkin, *Cats*, p.182.
5 Aristotle, *Historia Animalium* (4th century BC), trans. A. L. Peck (Cambridge, MA, 1965), vol. II, pp. 103, 105.
6 Plutarch, 'Isis and Osiris', in *Moralia*, trans. Frank Cole Babbitt (Cambridge, MA, 1957), vol. V, pp. 149–51; Claire Necker, *The Natural History of Cats* (South Brunswick, NJ, 1970), p. 82.
7 Pliny the Elder, *Natural History* (1st century AD), trans. H. Rackham (Cambridge, MA, 1956), vol. VIII, p. 223; Palladius, *The Fourteen Books of Palladius Rutilius Taurus Aemilianus, on Agriculture*, trans. T. Owen (London, 1807), p. 162.
8 'Cat', in *Encyclopedia Iranica* (1992), vol. V, p. 74; *Shah-nama of Firdaosi*, trans. Bahman Sohrab Surti (Secunderabad, Andrah

Pradesh, India, 1988), vol. VII, pp. 1560–63; Abbas Daneshvari, *Animal Symbolism in Warqa Wa Gulshah* (Oxford, 1986), pp. 36, 39–40.

9 Chang Tsu, 'The Empress's Cat', Wang Chih, 'Chang Tuan's Cats', in Felicity Bast, ed., *The Poetical Cat* (New York, 1995), pp. 21, 87.

10 'Cats', 'Sarashina nikki', *Kodansha Encyclopedia of Japan* (1983), vol. I, p. 251, vol. VII, p. 21; Murasaki Shikibu, *The Tale of Genji*, trans. Arthur Waley (New York, 1960), pp. 647, 648.

11 Martin R. Clutterbuck, *The Legend of Siamese Cats* (Bangkok, 1998), p. 57.

12 *Ancient Laws and Institutes of Wales; comprising Laws supposed to be enacted by Howel the Good* (1841), pp. 135–6, 355.

13 Dominique Buisson, *Le Chat Vu par les Peintres: Inde, Corée, Chine, Japon* (Lausanne, 1988), p. 32.

14 Aesop, *Fables*, trans S. A. Handford (Harmondsworth, 1964); *Pancatantra, The Book of India's Folk Wisdom*, trans. Patrick Olivelle (Oxford, 1977), Bk III, Sub-story 2.2.

15 In Joyce Carol Oates and Daniel Halperin, eds, *The Sophisticated Cat* (New York, 1992).

16 In Frank Brady and Martin Price, eds, *English Prose and Poetry 1660–1800* (New York, 1961), p. 537.

17 In Claire Necker, ed., *Supernatural Cats* (Garden City, NY, 1972).

18 Geoffrey Chaucer, *The Poetical Works*, ed. F. N. Robinson (Boston, 1933), p. 113; Bartholomew Anglicus, *Medieval Lore . . . Gleanings from the Encyclopedia of Bartholomew Anglicus* (c. 1250), ed. Robert Steele (London, 1893), pp. 134–5; G. R. Owst, *Literature and Pulpit in Medieval England* (Oxford, 1966), p. 389.

19 William Shakespeare, *The Merchant of Venice*, IV.i.55, *Much Ado about Nothing*, I.i.254–5, *A Midsummer Night's Dream*, III.ii.259, *The Rape of Lucrece*, 554–5, *Macbeth*, I.vii.44–5.

20 D. R. Guttery, *The Great Civil War in Midland Parishes: The People Pay* (Birmingham, 1951), p. 38; A. Gibbons, *Ely Episcopal Records* (Lincoln, 1891), p. 88.

21 Thomas Aquinas, *Summa Theologica* (1265–74), trans. Laurence Shapcote (Chicago, 1990), vol. II, pp. 297, 502–3; René Descartes,

Discourse on Method (1637), ed. and trans. Paul J. Olscamp
(Indianapolis, 1965), p. 121; letters to Mersenne, *Oeuvres*, ed.
Charles Adam and Paul Tannery (Paris, 1899), vol. III, p. 85.

22 Karen Armstrong, *Muhammad: A Biography of the Prophet* (San
Francisco, 1992), p. 231; *Sahih Bukhari* 1.12.712; *Sunan Abu-Dawud*
1.75, 1.76 (from website www.usc.edu/dept/MSA/reference/
searchhadith); Annemarie Schimmel's introduction to Lorraine
Chittock, *Cats of Cairo: Egypt's Enduring Legacy* (New York, 1999),
pp. 6–7, 63.

23 *Guardian*, no. 61 (1713), in Alexander Pope, *Works*, ed. Whitwell
Elwin and William John Courthope (New York, 1967), vol. X, p. 516.

24 Edward Moore, *Fables for the Ladies* (1744) (Haverhill, 1805), p. 31.

25 St George Mivart, *The Cat: An Introduction to the Study of Backboned
Animals, Especially Mammals* (New York, 1881), p. 1; Thorstein
Veblen, *Theory of the Leisure Class* (1899), in Claire Necker, ed.,
Cats and Dogs (South Brunswick, NJ, 1969), pp. 293–4; Edward G.
Fairholme and Wellesley Pain, *A Century of Work for Animals: The
History of the RSPCA, 1824–1924* (London, 1924), pp. 94–5.

2 THE MAGIC OF CATS, EVIL AND GOOD

1 Joyce Carol Oates and Daniel Halperin, eds, *The Sophisticated Cat*
(New York, 1992), p. 244.

2 Russell Hope Robbins, *The Encyclopedia of Witchcraft and
Demonology* (New York, 1963), p. 489; Hamish Whyte, ed., *The
Scottish Cat* (Aberdeen, 1987), pp. 51–3; Elizabeth Gaskell, *North
and South* (Harmondsworth, 1970), p. 477.

3 In Katharine M. Briggs, *Nine Lives: The Folklore of Cats* (New York,
1980).

4 Robbins, *Encyclopedia*, pp. 89–91.

5 George Lyman Kittredge, *Witchcraft in Old and New England* (New
York, 1958), p. 177; John Putnam Demos, *Entertaining Satan: Witchcraft and Culture in Early New England* (Oxford, 1982), pp. 141, 147.

6 In Claire Necker, ed., *Supernatural Cats* (Garden City, NY, 1972).

7 In F. Hadland Davis, *Myths and Legends of Japan* (Singapore,

1989), pp. 265–8.

8　Dominique Buisson, *Le Chat Vu par les Peintres: Inde, Corée, Chine, Japon* (Lausanne, 1988), pp. 114–17.

9　In Lafcadio Hearn, *Japanese Fairy Tales* (New York, 1953).

10　Kathleen Alpar-Ashton, ed., *Histoires et Légendes du Chat* (1973), pp. 25, 41–2. The story of Jean Foucault is in Alpar-Ashton; 'Owney' is in William Butler Yeats, ed., *Fairy and Folk Tales of Ireland* (New York, 1973).

11　John Seidensticker and Susan Lumpkin, *Cats: Smithsonian Answer Book* (Washington, DC, 2004), p. 189; Ambroise Paré, *Collected Works*, trans. Thomas Johnson (New York, 1968), p. 804.

12　Edward Topsell, *The History of Four-Footed Beasts and Serpents and Insects* (New York, 1967), vol. I, pp. 81, 83.

13　Joseph Addison, *The Spectator*, ed. G. Gregory Smith, Number 117 (London, 1950), vol. I, p. 357.

14　Scott in Robert Byrne and Teressa Skelton, *Cat Scan: All the Best from the Literature of Cats* (New York, 1983), p. 46; Edgar Allan Poe, 'Instinct vs. Reason', in *Collected Works*, ed. Thomas Ollive Mabbott (Cambridge, MA, 1978), p. 479.

15　Charles Pierre Baudelaire, *Oeuvres complètes*, preface by Théophile Gautier (Paris, 1868), vol. I, pp. 33–5.

16　H. P. Lovecraft, *Something about Cats and Other Pieces*, ed. August Derleth (Sauk City, WI, 1949), pp. 4, 8.

17　Poe, *Works*, p. 859.

18　Charles Dickens, *Bleak House* (1853) (New York, 1977), p. 130.

19　Charles Dickens, *Dombey and Son* (1848) (London, 1899), vol. II, p. 40.

20　Émile Zola, *Thérèse Raquin* (1867), trans. George Holden (Harmondsworth, 1962), pp. 68–9, 166.

21　Judy Fireman, ed., *Cat Catalog: The Ultimate Cat Book* (New York, 1976), p. 40; Fred Gettings, *The Secret Lore of the Cat* (New York, 1989), pp. 74–6; David Greene, *Your Incredible Cat: Understanding the Secret Powers of Your Pet* (Garden City, NY, 1986), pp. 48–50.

22　Alpar-Ashton, *Histoires et Légendes*, pp. 140–42.

23　Briggs, *Nine Lives*, pp. 17–18.

24 In Alpar-Ashton, *Histoires et Légendes.*

25 Iona and Peter Opie, eds, *The Classic Fairy Tales* (London, 1974),
p. 113; Jacob Grimm, *Teutonic Mythology*, trans. James Steven
Stallybrass (New York, 1966), vol. II, p. 503.

26 Alan Pate, 'Maneki Neko, Feline Fact and Fiction', *Daruma:
Japanese Art and Antiques Magazine*, XI (Summer 1996), pp. 27–9.

27 Buisson, *Le Chat*, p. 11.

28 Martin R. Clutterbuck, *The Legend of Siamese Cats* (Bangkok,
1998), pp. 29, 53.

29 Stories of Usugomo and of the cat who helped the fishmonger in
Pate, 'Maneki Neko'; 'The Boy Who Drew Cats' in Hearn, *Japanese
Fairy Tales*; story of Okesa in Juliet Piggott, ed., *Japanese
Mythology* (New York, 1969); Thai story told me by Ms Sirikanya
B. Schaeffer.

3 CHERISHED INMATES OF HOME AND SALON

1 'Pangur Ban' in Felicity Bast, ed., *The Poetical Cat* (New York,
1995), pp. 28–9; epitaph on Belaud in Dorothy Foster, ed., *In
Praise of Cats* (New York, 1974), pp. 115–17; Michel Eyquem de
Montaigne, 'Apology of Raymond Sebond' (1580), *Essays*, trans.
John Florio (London, 1946), vol. II, p. 142.

2 Marie d'Aulnoy, *Les Contes des fées* (Paris, 1881), vol. II, p. 101.
'The Little White Cat' is in Kathleen Alpar-Ashton, ed., *Histoires et
Légendes du Chat* (1973).

3 Christabel Aberconway, *A Dictionary of Cat Lovers XV Century
B.C.–XX Century A.D.* (London, 1968), pp.124, 138–9; Leonora
Rosenfield, *From Beast-Machine to Man-Machine* (New York, 1941),
pp. 161–4; François-Augustin Paradis de Moncrif, *Moncrif's Cats*,
trans. Reginald Bretnor (New York, 1965), pp. 130–35; Horace
Walpole, *Correspondence*, ed. W. S. Lewis (New Haven, 1937–83),
vol. XII, p. 121, vol. XXXI, p. 54.

4 Richard Steele, *The Tatler*, ed. Donald F. Bond (Oxford, 1987), vol.
II, p. 177; Delille in Aberconway, *Dictionary*, p. 119; Stuart Piggott,
William Stukeley, an Eighteenth-Century Antiquarian (London,

1985), p. 124; Christopher Smart, *Collected Poems*, ed. Norman
Callan (London, 1949), vol. I, pp. 312–13.

5 James Boswell, *Life of Johnson*, ed. R. W. Chapman (London, 1953),
p. 1217.

6 James Boswell, *Boswell on the Grand Tour: Germany and
Switzerland*, ed. Frederick A. Pottle (New York, 1953), p. 261.

7 Georges Louis Leclerc Buffon, *Natural History, General and
Particular* (1749–67), trans. William Smellie (London, 1791), vol.
IV, pp. 2–4, 49–50, 52–3.

8 'Poor Matthias', in *Poets of the English Language*, ed. W. H. Auden
and Norman Holmes Pearson (London, 1952), vol. V, p. 247;
Aberconway, *Dictionary*, p. 22; Charles Dudley Warner, *The
Writings* (Hartford, 1904), pp. 127–8; Thomas Hardy, *Selected
Poems*, ed. G. M. Young (London, 1950), p. 140.

9 Aberconway, *Dictionary*, pp. 249–50, 372; Théophile Gautier,
Complete Works, trans. and ed. F. C. De Sumichrast (London,
1909), pp. 289–92.

10 Joyce Carol Oates and Daniel Halperin, *The Sophisticated Cat*
(New York, 1992), pp. 360–61.

11 *The Gospel of the Holy Twelve*, trans. by A Disciple of the Master
(Issued by the Order of At-One-Ment, n.d.), note to ch. 4, verse 4.

12 Toni Morrison, *The Bluest Eye* (New York, 1970), p. 70.

13 Brian Reade, *Louis Wain* (London, 1972), p. 5.

14 Paul Gallico, *Honorable Cat* (New York, 1972), p. 7; Winifred
Carrière, *Cats Twenty-Four Hours a Day* (New York, 1967), p. 8; the
Warner story is in Beth Brown, ed., *All Cats Go to Heaven: An
Anthology of Stories about Cats* (New York, 1960); Susan DeVore
Williams, ed., *Cats: The Love They Give Us* (Old Tappan, NJ, 1988);
Paul Corey, *Do Cats Think?* (Secaucus, NJ, 1977), p.10.

15 Kathleen Kete, *The Beast in the Boudoir: Petkeeping in Nineteenth-
Century Paris* (Berkeley, CA, 1994), pp.127–8.

16 Official websites of the American Cat Fanciers' Association and
the Governing Council of the Cat Fancy; Harrison Weir, *Our Cats
and All about Them* (Boston, 1889), p. 5; Gordon Stables, *Cats:
Handbook to Their Classification and Diseases* (1876) (London,

1897), pp. 8–9, 13–14, 29–30; Elizabeth Hamilton, *Cats: A Celebration* (New York, 1979), p. 117.

17 Ibid.

4 CATS AND WOMEN

1 Kathleen Kete, *The Beast in the Boudoir: Petkeeping in Nineteenth-Century Paris* (Berkeley, CA, 1994), pp. 119–21.

2 Émile Zola, *Thérèse Raquin* (1867), trans. George Holden (Harmondsworth, 1962), pp. 37–8.

3 Verlaine's poem in Felicity Bast, ed., *The Poetical Cat* (New York, 1995); Lucas in Robert Byrne and Teressa Skelton, *Cat Scan: All the Best from the Literature of Cats* (New York, 1983), p. 59.

4 Guy de Maupassant, *Complete Short Stories* (Garden City, NY, 1955), pp. 659–61.

5 Sigmund Freud, 'On Narcissism: An Introduction' (1914), in *Collected Papers* (New York, 1959).

6 Louis Allen and Jean Wilson, eds, *Lafcadio Hearn: Japan's Great Interpreter* (Sandgate, Kent, 1992), p. 69.

7 Sylvia Townsend Warner, *Lolly Willowes and Mr Fortune's Maggot* (1926) (New York, 1966), p. 136.

8 Joyce Carol Oates and Daniel Halperin, eds, *The Sophisticated Cat* (New York, 1992), pp. 208–9, 227.

9 Maitland in Claire Necker, ed., *Cats and Dogs* (South Brunswick, NJ, 1969), pp. 128–31, 139; Philip Hamerton, *Chapters on Animals* (Boston, 1882), pp. 47, 49, 51.

10 Michael and Mollie Hardwick, eds, *The Charles Dickens Encyclopedia* (New York, 1973), p. 452.

11 'mehitabel and her kittens'; both poems in Don Marquis, *The Life and Times of Archy and Mehitabel* (1927) (Garden City, NY, 1950), pp. 77–8, 216–17.

12 Ambrose Bierce, *The Collected Writings* (New York, 1946), p. 388; Jung in Barbara Hannah, *The Cat, Dog, and Horse Lectures* (Wilmette, IL, 1992), p. 64.

13 Jeff Reid, *Cat-Dependent No More! Learning to Live Cat-Free in a Cat-Filled World* (New York, 1991), pp. 38, 107, 126; Robert

Daphne, *How to Kill Your Girlfriend's Cat* (New York, 1988) is
unpaged.

14 Paul Gallico, *The Silent Miaow: A Manual for Kittens, Strays, and
Homeless Cats* (New York, 1964), pp. 38–40; Kinky Friedman,
Greenwich Killing Time (New York, 1986), p. 122; Paul Gallico,
Honorable Cat (New York, 1972), p.14; Konrad Lorenz, *Man Meets
Dog* (Baltimore, 1967), pp. 180–81.

15 Keith Pratt and Richard Rutt, *Korea: A Historical and Cultural
Dictionary* (Richmond, Surrey, 1999), p. 37.

5 CATS APPRECIATED AS INDIVIDUALS

1 Christabel Aberconway, *A Dictionary of Cat Lovers XV Century
B.C.–XX Century A.D.* (London, 1968), p. 96; Claire Necker, ed., *Cats
and Dogs* (South Brunswick, NJ, 1969), pp. 146–8; Caroline
Thomas Harnsberger, ed., *Everyone's Mark Twain* (South
Brunswick, NJ, 1972), pp. 68–9.

2 Rudyard Kipling, *Just So Stories* (1902) (New York, 1991), p. 105.

3 Seon Manley and Gogo Lewis, eds, *Cat-Encounters: A Cat Lover's
Anthology* (New York, 1979), p. 70.

4 Beth Brown, ed., *All Cats Go to Heaven: An Anthology of Stories
about Cats* (New York, 1960), p. 36.

5 Carter's story is in Joyce Carol Oates and Daniel Halperin, eds,
The Sophisticated Cat (New York, 1992).

6 Natsume Soseki, *I Am a Cat: A Novel* (1905–6), trans. Katsue
Shibata and Motonari Kai (New York, 1961), pp. 106, 151, 183–4,
245, 431.

7 Robertson Davies, *The Table Talk of Samuel Marchbanks* (Toronto,
1949), p. 187; 'Tobermory' in *The Short Stories of Saki* (New York,
1930).

8 'Fluffy' is in Michel Parry, ed., *Beware of the Cat: Stories of Feline
Fantasy and Horror* (New York, 1973); 'Miss Paisley's Cat', in
Cynthia Manson, ed., *Mystery Cats* (New York, 1991); 'Smith', in
Claire Necker, ed., *Supernatural Cats* (Garden City, NY, 1972).

9 Oates and Halperin, *Sophisticated Cat*, p. xii.

10 Robert A. Heinlein, *The Door into Summer* (New York, 1957), pp. 42–3; John Dann MacDonald, *The House Guests* (Garden City, NY, 1965), pp. 178–9.

11 Dominique Buisson, *Le Chat Vu par les Peintres: Inde, Corée, Chine, Japon* (Lausanne, 1988), pp. 32–3; Daisetz T. Suzuki, *Zen and Japanese Culture* (New York, 1959), pp. 428–33.

12 Haruki Murakami, *The Wind-Up Bird Chronicle* (1994), trans. Jay Rubin (New York, 1997), 381–2, 430; Haruki Murakami, *Kafka on the Shore* (2002), trans. Philip Gabriel (New York, 2005), pp. 44, 45, 48, 71–3, 75, 88, 196–7.

13 Hall's story in Radclyffe Hall, *Miss Ogilvy Finds Herself* (New York, 1934); Lessing's in Doris Lessing, *Temptations of Jack Orkney and Other Stories* (New York, 1972).

14 May Sarton, *The Fur Person* (New York, 1957), pp. 104–5.

15 Louise Patteson, *Pussy Meow: The Autobiography of a Cat* (Philadelphia, 1901), p. 106.

16 Robert Westall, *Blitzcat* (New York, 1989), pp. 7–8.

6 THE FASCINATION OF PARADOX

1 John Seidensticker and Susan Lumpkin, *Cats: Smithsonian Answer Book* (Washington, DC, 2004), p. 205; pro-research and anti-vivisectionist web sites: Foundation for Biomedical Research (www.fbresearch.org/education), University of Arizona course on Dogs and Cats in Biomedical Research (www.ahsc.arizona.edu/uac/notes/classes/dogsbioo1), Research Defence Society, www.vivisectioninfo.org/cat.html, www.mar-chofcrimes.com/facts.html; personal communications from Drs Kristina Narfstrom of the University of Missouri and Ralph Nelson of the National Institutes of Health.

2 Peter Singer, *Animal Liberation: A New Ethics for Our Treatment of Animals* (New York, 1975), pp. 52–3, 58–9.

3 For UK statistics, www.scotland.gov.uk/library5/environment; for US statistics, http://www.petfoodinstitute.org/reference.

4 A. L. Rowse, *A Quartet of Cornish Cats* (London, 1986), pp. 30–32.

5 Christopher Smart, *Collected Poems*, ed. Norman Callan (London, 1949), vol. I, p. 313; Mark Twain, *Pudd'n-head Wilson* (1894) (New York, 1964), pp. 21–2; Joanna Baillie, 'The Kitten', in Dorothy Foster, *In Praise of Cats* (New York, 1974), pp. 54–7.
6 Colette, *Creatures Great and Small*, trans. Enid McLeod (New York, 1951), p. 242.
7 Kenneth Lillington, ed., *Nine Lives: An Anthology of Poetry and Prose Concerning Cats* (London, 1977), p.108.

Bibliography

Aberconway, Christabel, ed., *A Dictionary of Cat Lovers xv Century b.c.–xx Century a.d.* (London, 1968)

Alpar-Ashton, Kathleen, ed., *Histoires et Légendes du Chat* (1973)

Bast, Felicity, ed., *The Poetical Cat* (New York, 1995)

Briggs, Katharine M., *Nine Lives: The Folklore of Cats* (New York, 1980)

Buffon, Georges Louis Leclerc, *Natural History, General and Particular* (1749–67), trans. William Smellie (London, 1791)

Byrne, Robert, and Teressa Skelton, eds, *Cat Scan: All the Best from the Literature of Cats* (New York, 1983)

Buisson, Dominique, *Le Chat Vu par les Peintres: Inde, Corée, Chine, Japon* (Lausanne, 1988)

Clutterbuck, Martin R. *The Legend of Siamese Cats* (Bangkok, 1998)

Foster, Dorothy, ed., *In Praise of Cats* (New York, 1974)

Foucart-Walter, Elizabeth, and Pierre Rosenberg, *The Painted Cat: The Cat in Western Painting from the Fifteenth to the Twentieth Century* (New York, 1988)

Holland, Barbara. *The Name of the Cat* (New York, 1988)

Leyhausen, Paul. *Cat Behavior: The Predatory and Social Behavior of Domestic and Wild Cats*, trans. Barbara A. Tonkin (New York, 1979)

Malek, Jaromir, *The Cat in Ancient Egypt* (London, 1993)

Mivart, St, George, *The Cat: An Introduction to the Study of Backboned Animals, Especially Mammals* (New York, 1881)

Moncrif, François-Augustin Paradis de, *Moncrif's Cats*, trans. Reginald Bretnor (New York, 1965)

Necker, Claire, ed., *Cats and Dogs* (South Brunswick, NJ, 1969)

—, ed., *Supernatural Cats* (Garden City, NY, 1972)

New Yorker Book of Cat Cartoons, The (New York, 1990)

Oates, Joyce Carol, and Daniel Halperin, eds, *The Sophisticated Cat* (New York, 1992)

O'Neill, John P. *Metropolitan Cats* (New York, 1981)

Parry, Michel, ed., *Beware of the Cat: Stories of Feline Fantasy and Horror* (New York, 1973)

Ritvo, Harriet, *The Animal Estate: The English and Other Creatures in the Victorian Age* (Cambridge, MA, 1987)

Rogers, Katharine M., *The Cat and the Human Imagination: Feline Images from Bast to Garfield* (Ann Arbor, 1998)

Sarton, May *The Fur Person* (New York, 1957)

Seidensticker, John, and Susan Lumpkin. *Cats: Smithsonian Answer Book* (Washington, DC, 2004)

Thomas, Keith. *Man and the Natural World: A History of the Modern Sensibility* (New York, 1983)

Warren, Rosalind, ed., *Kitty Libber: Cat Cartoons by Women* (Freedom, CA, 1992)

Weir, Harrison, *Our Cats and All about Them* (Boston, 1889)

Whyte, Hamish, ed., *The Scottish Cat* (Aberdeen, 1987)

Associations and Websites

AMERICAN ASSOCIATION FOR LABORATORY ANIMAL SCIENCE
http://www.aalas.org
Promotes responsible use and care of cats and other laboratory
animals in order to benefit both people and animals.

AMERICAN ASSOCIATION OF FELINE PRACTITIONERS
http://www.aafponline.org
An association of veterinary doctors and students that seeks to
raise the standards of feline medicine by sharing knowledge,
sponsoring continuing education and encouraging interest in
feline practice.

AMERICAN HUMANE ASSOCIATION
http://www.americanhumane.org
The American Humane Association, along with the American
Society for Prevention of Cruelty to Animals and the Humane
Society of the United States, works for the welfare of cats and
other animals.

CAT FANCIERS' ASSOCIATION
http://www.cfainc.org
The Cat Fanciers' Association promotes and regulates pedigree cat
breeding and showing in the United States by setting standards,
registering pedigree cats and producing shows. It also funds

research aimed to improve feline health through the Winn Feline Foundation. Its website provides information on cat shows and cat breeds, with pictures of prizewinning cats. It also presents the CFA's position on current legislative issues involving cats and a section on cat care that includes both research reports from the Winn Foundation and general articles such as 'Myths and Facts about Cats'.

CATS INTERNATIONAL
http://www.catsinternational.org
Dedicated to helping people better understand their feline companions. Its website provides a large collection of useful articles on feline psychology and solutions to behaviour problems. The organization also maintains a Behaviour Hotline.

CATS PROTECTION
http://www.cats.org.uk
This is the leading feline welfare charity in the United Kingdom. It rescues and finds homes for cats and kittens through a network of adoption centres, and it provides information about cat care and responsible ownership through a helpline, educational materials for schools and its website. The website offers articles on cat care and health that can be downloaded, as well as a gallery of photographs and games.

CAT WRITERS' ASSOCIATION, INC.
http://www.catwriters.org
Organization of writers that encourages writing about cats by its newsletter, mailing list and competitive awards.

GOVERNING COUNCIL OF THE CAT FANCY
http://ourworld.compuserve.com/homepages/GCCF__CATS
Uniting the local cat clubs in the United Kingdom, the Governing Council of the Cat Fancy regulates the breeding and showing of pedigree cats by keeping registers and licensing cat shows. It

declares its strong interest in the welfare of non-pedigree as well as pedigree cats and supports research on feline health.

Searching for 'Cats' in the Yahoo directory (http://dir.yahoo.com) and then clicking on Cats under Related Directory Categories yields a list of several hundred websites on cats, dealing with care of cats and kittens, breeds, mythology and folklore, history, anatomy (on the college level), health, remedies for problem behaviour, etc. and offering beautiful, cute or humorous pictures.

Acknowledgements

I would like to thank the well-informed and helpful reference librarians in the Main Reading Room and the Asian Division of the Library of Congress and in the Arthur M. Sackler Gallery of the Smithsonian Institution, who patiently answered questions and directed me to valuable sources. I am especially grateful to Ms Sirikanya B. Schaeffer, a fellow cat enthusiast, who drew my attention to the *Tamra Maeo Thai* manuscript in the Asian Division. In addition, Drs Pierre Comizzoli, Kristina Narfstrom and Ralph Nelson graciously enlightened me about research on cats.

My husband, Kenneth, has tirelessly exerted his skills and his patience to photograph many of the images in this book. *Cat* would never have been completed without his support and technical expertise.

Photo Acknowledgements

The author and publishers wish to express their thanks to the below sources of illustrative material and/or permission to reproduce it. (Some sources uncredited in the captions for reasons of brevity are also given below.)

Photo © 2006 Artists Rights Society (ARS) New York/ADAGP, Paris: p. 125; Bayerische Staatsgemäldesammlungen, Munich: p. 41; Bibliothèque Nationale de France, Paris: pp. 27, 90 (Département des Estampes et Photographie), 115, 119; British Library, London: pp. 35 (Add. MSS 42130, fol. 190r), 145; British Library, London (Add. MSS 11283, fol. 15r); British Museum, London: p. 16; Buffon, *l'Histoire Naturelle* (vol. XXIV): p. 87; The Corcoran Gallery of Art, Washington, DC: p. 128 (Museum Purchase, William A. Clark Fund 23.4); J. Paul Getty Museum, Los Angeles, California: p. 84 (84.PA.665); Graphische Sammlung Albertina, Vienna: p. 131; photo © 1994 by Herblock in The *Washington Post*, p. 168 (Herb Block Foundation); photo Bob Koestler, Saroko Cattery: p. 112; photo Michael R. Leaman/Reaktion Books: p. 111 (left); Library of Congress, Washington, DC: pp. 76, 77 (courtesy of the Asian Division), 83 (photo T.W. Ingersoll, Prints and Photographs Division, LC-USZ-62-100476), 98 left (Prints and Photographs Division, LC-USZC4-11932), 98 right (Prints and Photographs Division, Theatrical Poster Collection, LC-USZ6-441), 99 (Prints and Photographs Division, LC-USZC4-5166), 103 (Prints and Photographs Division, LC-USZC62-93145), 108 (Prints and Photographs Division, National Photo Company Collection, LC-USZ62-106978), 134 (Prints and Photographs Division, Theatrical Poster Collection, LC-USZC4-12408-12410), 135 (Prints

Index